PICTURE BOOKS FOR THE LITERACY HOUR

ACTIVITIES FOR PRIMARY TEACHERS

EDITED BY

GUY MERCHANT AND HUW THOMAS

This book has been produced by the Centre for English in Education at the School of Education, Sheffield Hallam University

Contributions from: Kath Cooper, Paul Dickinson, Jackie Marsh, Jim McDonagh, Jeff Wilkinson
Artwork by Jan Smith

David Fulton Publishers
London

David Fulton Publishers Ltd
Ormond House, 26–27 Boswell Street, London WC1N 3JD
Web address: http://www.fultonbooks.co.uk

First published in Great Britain in 1999 by David Fulton Publishers
Reprinted 2000

Note: The rights of Guy Merchant and Huw Thomas
to be identified as the editors of this work has been asserted by
them in accordance with the Copyright, Design and Patents Act 1988.

British Library Cataloguing in Publication Data
A catalogue record for this book is available from the British Library

ISBN 1–85346–627–1

Typeset by Textype Typesetters, Cambridge
Printed in Great Britain by Bell and Bain Ltd, Glasgow

Contents

Acknowledgements

Acknowledgement is made to the following publishers for permission to use copyright material:

Walker Books Limited for *Where's my Teddy* by Jez Alborough, *We're Going on a Bear Hunt* by Michael Rosen and Helen Oxenbury, *Handa's Surprise* by Eileen Browne, *Let the Lynx Come In* by Jonathan London and Patrick Benson, *Captain Abdul's Pirate School* by Colin McNaughton, *Have You Seen Who's Just Moved Next Door to Us?* By Colin McNaughton, *The Egyptian News* by Scott Steedman, *Greek Myths for Young Children* by Marcia Williams, *Mr William Shakespeare's Plays* by Marcia Williams, *Can't You Sleep Little Bear?* by Martin Waddell and Barbara Firth, *Owl Babies* by Martin Waddell and Patrick Benson and *Farmer Duck* by Martin Waddell and Helen Oxenbury.

Penguin Books Ltd for *Something Else* by Kathryn Cave and Chris Riddell, *It Was a Dark and Stormy Night* by Janet and Allan Ahlberg and *Always Adam* by Sheldon Oberman and Ted Lewin.

Random House UK Limited for *The Whales' Song* by Dyan Sheldon and Gary Blythe (published by Hutchinson), *Zoo* by Anthony Browne (published by Julia McRae) and *Dr Dog* by Babette Cole (published by Jonathan Cape).

Hodder and Stoughton Limited for *The Blue Balloon* by Mick Inkpen.

John Murray (Publishers) Ltd for *The Highwayman* by Alfred Noyes and Charles Keeping from his *Collected Poems*.

Oxford University Press for *Snow White in New York* by Fiona French.

Egmont Children's Books Limited for *One Smiling Grandma*, text © 1992 Anne Marie Linden, illustrations © 1992 Lynne Russell, published by Heinemann Young Books and Mammoth, imprints of Egmont Children's Books Limited.

Pavilion Books Ltd for *Seasons of Splendour* by Madhur Jaffrey.

Transworld Publishers for *Voices in the Park* by Anthony Browne.

Notes on the contributors

Kath Cooper has 12 years' teaching experience at Key Stages 1 and 2. She was in the first cohort of teachers to be trained by the National Literacy Project. She is currently seconded to the Centre for English in Education, where she is developing her interest in literacy across the curriculum.

Paul Dickinson is a Senior Lecturer and coordinates the Secondary PGCE course in English. He was formerly Head of Upper School English at a comprehensive school. He is particularly interested in subject mentoring in English and specialises in the field of Key Stage 3 Literacy.

Jackie Marsh is a Principal Lecturer in primary English working on the Initial Teacher Education programme. Her research interests are in the role of popular culture in early years language and literacy development. Her publications include *Co-ordinating Primary Language and Literacy* and *Desirable Literacies*.

Jim McDonagh works in the Centre for English in Education and has a particular interest in the teaching of English as an Additional Language. He taught for a number of years in multilingual primary schools. His research interests are in teachers' subject knowledge.

Guy Merchant is Head of the Centre for English in Education coordinating the team's in-service provision and the MA (Language and Literacy). His research interests are in the field of early literacy development in multilingual contexts. He has written articles and books on literacy development. His most recent publication is *Co-ordinating Primary Language and Literacy* and *Desirable Literacies*.

Huw Thomas teaches at Springfield School, a multicultural, inner-city school in Sheffield. He is author of a number of titles on literacy, including *Reading and Responding to Fiction* (1998), and is a regular contributor to the *TES*, *Literacy and Learning* and *Junior Education*.

Jeff Wilkinson lectures in English in Education and has extensive experience of initial and in-service training at both primary and secondary levels. He has a particular interest in language study and its relationship to the development of reading and writing skills. He has written and co-authored several books and articles on the teaching of English and is currently researching the teaching of grammar in primary and secondary schools.

Introduction

Over the last 30 years, growth in the popularity and provision of books for children has been remarkable. The quality and inventiveness of children's authors and illustrators have led some to think of the picture book as a new art form. Our book began as a celebration of some of this work and it concentrates on the potential that picture books have for the teaching and learning of literacy.

Our aim in writing this book is to encourage colleagues to take a closer look at some of their favourite picture books and to see how they can be used as a starting point for enjoyable and challenging literacy work in primary classrooms. We believe that teachers do not need to rely on schemes to structure their English curriculum. With this in mind we have selected 24 popular titles and have looked at them in terms of their potential for delivering exciting text-, sentence- and word-level work.

Inevitably our selection of picture books is limited. There are many titles, authors and illustrators we could have included but we have been forced to make some hard choices. The titles we use cover both Key Stages and have been used extensively by the authors and by our colleagues in primary schools. They are, with one exception, narrative in form, but give some impression of the range and variety within this category.

Reading this book

We intend this book to be used as a resource, and anticipate that many readers will be most interested in our commentaries on the picture books (contained in Chapters 3–7) and the accompanying photocopiable activity sheets. Picture books we have used have been divided into five categories. These categories are used as chapter headings ('Looking at how stories work'; 'Entering imaginary worlds'; 'Learning about ourselves and others'; 'Exploring feelings'; and 'Thinking about issues'). Of course, most of the titles would fit several of the categories, but we have organised them according to the ways in which we have read them and used them with children. To some extent, then, the categorisation is rather arbitrary, yet we hope that readers will find this a useful starting point, perhaps developing a more flexible approach as they become more familiar with the texts.

- **Chapter 1** provides the reader with a rationale for the use of high quality picture books and examines how they promote and support an understanding and enjoyment of literacy.
- **Chapter 2** looks at the different ways in which reading picture books can be organised in primary classrooms. Our intention here is to demonstrate how picture

books can be used in the Literacy Hour and also to show how such work can be built on in other areas of the curriculum and at other times during the school day.

- **Chapter 3** focuses on six titles which we have used to develop work examining how stories work. These titles have been particularly useful in work on story structure, story elements and common features of narrative.
- **Chapter 4** focuses on picture books which are useful in looking at fantasy and imaginary worlds. We have selected a further six titles to accompany this theme.
- **Chapter 5** looks at stories that can be a vehicle for understanding the cultural and social lives of ourselves and others. Here we have chosen four titles.
- **Chapter 6** includes four titles we have found particularly helpful in exploring feelings and emotions.
- **Chapter 7** addresses the role of picture books in looking at wider social and environmental issues.
- **Chapter 8** discusses ways of building up picture book resources and offers guidance on how to plan from texts. There is also advice on how to build up your own bank of picture book resources at school.

We hope that this book is of practical benefit to teachers, coordinators and consultants – indeed all those who wish to develop an interest and enjoyment in reading using picture books. We would like to thank those teachers and student-teachers from Sheffield and the surrounding region who have shared their ideas and enthusiasm for using these picture books. We are particularly indebted to Pauleen Flannery, the English Inspector for Doncaster LEA, for providing useful opportunities for working with both primary and secondary colleagues.

Finally, we would particularly like to hear from teachers who have tried out our ideas on these and other picture books. Please send your comments to:

The Picture Book Project
Centre for English in Education
College House
Collegiate Campus
Sheffield S10 2BP

1 Picture books in the primary classroom

'While illustrations are not always necessary or desirable in children's novels, they are an essential part of the picture book . . . the more rewarding examples of the genre show a complete integration of text and illustration, the book shaped and designed as a whole, produced by a combination of finely balanced verbal and visual qualities.

(Whalley and Chester 1988, p. 216)

This chapter looks at the specific qualities of the picture book and begins with an appreciation of the genre as a distinct category of children's literature, showing how children bring print and visual awareness to their reading of such texts. We then address a number of questions related to the use of picture books. First we look at the legacy of the 'real books' debate as a way of identifying the importance of including picture books in the range of resource material in classrooms. Then we explore how picture books manage to cater for the varied interests of children and adults. This leads to a discussion of how we are drawn into such texts and become active readers, learning with and learning from picture books. We conclude with a look at book formats, the importance of sharing and negotiating meaning and a discussion of the role of the big book in the classroom setting.

Image and print

In their lives at home and in educational settings, children will be introduced to print in a variety of forms from an early age. They will also be growing up in an environment that is rich in visual images. As children learn to take meaning from text they will become increasingly sensitive to how print and other visual information can interact. On television screens, on advertising hoardings, in supermarkets and on public transport, image and print are characteristically seen together. Teachers who make use of these environmental texts are able to promote children's learning by building on their everyday experiences.

However, despite a healthy and growing interest in different kinds of literacy practices, book-based literacy remains a central part of curricular provision. Picture books provide a powerful introduction to the world of reading by combining children's sensitivity to the visual image with their growing knowledge of the printed word (Graham 1990). In many primary classrooms children's enthusiasm for the work of Jill Murphy or Anthony Browne has as much to do with an appreciation of their visual style as with the fictions they create. In fact it could be argued that the real fascination lies in the ways in which print and image interact – how they tell alternative stories or provide additional information.

Probably the picture book is best described as an art-form through which authors and illustrators communicate what concerns them and how they reflect on the experience of childhood. Producing a picture book is primarily a creative process; these texts provide a rich introduction to fictional characters in imagined settings and show children the possibilities of story and visual image as well as the enjoyment that can be derived from reading.

It is perhaps difficult to give a precise definition of the picture book. A wealth of well-illustrated children's literature is currently available, not all of which is easy to classify. Some titles, particularly those longer stories written for the older primary age range, communicate mostly through print, visual images being employed as accompanying illustration. Others inhabit a sort of border land. Jan Ormerod's illustrations undoubtedly add another dimension to *The Snow Maze* (by Jan Mark) and yet the book hardly classes as a picture book. Recent years have seen the emergence of lavishly illustrated information books for children – books in which the visual image has a central part to play. But, in the end, it seems to us that the defining feature of the picture book is the story that it tells and the ways in which it tells it. These books are narratives that are characterised by the dynamic relationship between print and visual image.

Are picture books real?

Several years ago the media contributed to a rather unsettling moral panic over the teaching of reading. We were told that teachers, in large numbers, had abandoned the 'tried and tested' structured approaches to teaching reading and were jumping onto the bandwagon of using 'real books'. This was, in fact, far from the truth but for one important aspect: teachers had begun to realise that children could learn as much, if not more, from books not primarily designed to teach reading – the so-called 'real books'. In many cases the rather ambiguous term 'real books' became synonymous with picture books.

Learning from picture books and learning to read with picture books remain important considerations in our provision of a range of resources in the primary classroom. As teachers become more familiar with planning to the National Literacy Strategy objectives, the opportunities for using good quality picture books are becoming apparent. Texts designed to teach the objectives are unlikely to have the same depth, or range of possibilities. As a recent contributor to *The Primary English Magazine* observes, 'The texts chosen need to help the teacher to deliver the objectives; but *much* more importantly they need to inspire reading' (Lambirth 1998, p. 29).

Who are they for?

It is sometimes argued that picture books are really written for adults – parents and teachers – rather than children, and certainly it seems that the best picture books do appeal to all ages. The important message here is to understand why they can be enjoyed by different age groups and how this can help the reading process.

. . . secretly
she dropped a
poisoned cherry in a
cocktail and handed
it to Snow White
with a smile.

(*From* Snow White in New
York *by Fiona French*)

Some of the best picture books can be described as being multi-layered, in that they carry a number of layers or levels of meaning. For instance, Allan and Janet Ahlberg's *Peepo!* is a simple rhyme about a day in the life of a family, focusing on the children's point of view. However, on closer inspection, the illustrations reveal that the day's events are set in a particular social and historical context (another layer of meaning). As we realise that the setting is wartime Britain, and that the father figure is a soldier, another layer of meanings is uncovered, leading us, perhaps, to reflect on disruption and discontinuity in family life. These different layers are embedded in the detail of illustration and text.

Most good picture books can be used effectively with older primary children. A relatively 'simple' text can be given a more searching reading in Key Stage 2 or even Key Stage 3. Usually the biggest barrier at this age is created by adults and children who associate picture books with early reading. The sort of narrative complexities we refer to in this discussion of picture books indicate the depth of analysis that is possible. Readers who have come to associate the number of chapters, the size of print or the thickness of the book with reading progress can be re-educated through sensitive teaching. One has only to look closely at *Snow White in New York* (French) to savour the rich intertextuality as the illustrations evoke a particular setting and the language a particular dialect as this traditional tale is reworked.

So, texts that are rich in meaning can capture the interest of adults and children alike. They can revisit them and learn something new each time they are read. And this means that adults will be motivated to share them with younger readers. Parents, teaching assistants in the classroom and older brothers and sisters will also be interested in what such a book holds for them.

In this way, picture books can be an influential means of building reading partnerships with parents. Rather than simply encouraging reading practice at home they can provide a context for exploring meanings at adult level as well. So, for example, the fascinating accounts of Friedberg and Segal (1997) illustrate how Mary Hoffman's *Amazing Grace* provided the context for African-American parents to discuss racism, role models, their own aspirations and their hopes for the younger generation. This is only possible because of the multi-layered nature of the picture book.

Do they hold our attention?

For children and adults, one of the attractions of contemporary picture books is the quality of presentation. Although colourful illustration and a clear typeface are not the only criteria for selecting books, technical advances in publishing and printing have undoubtedly provided wider choices for writers and illustrators, the best of whom know how to draw appropriately from the resources available to them.

And this morning, while I was taking it for a walk...

Reproduced from *THE BLUE BALLOON*, © Mick Inkpen,

A growing number of books incorporate sophisticated 'book technology' such as moving parts, see-through pages, pop-ups, lift-the-flaps and even electronic sounds and lights. Here, it is important to distinguish between gimmicks and features which seem to add to the meaning of the text. Books that illustrate this dimension include *Rainbow Fish*, in which reflective foil is used to add another dimension to the fish that is described, and *The Blue Balloon*, in which pages unfold allowing for illustration and print that extends the meaning of the text.

Some of the best picture books use humour, rhyme or dialogue to draw the reader in in a way that encourages us to think about and reflect upon our own experiences.

As we have seen, the subtleties of meaning are not always apparent until we re-read the text or look more closely at the visual images that accompany it. In successive readings we are likely to develop our response to the text and exchange our insights with children.

Authors also make careful use of language to invite us into their stories. This may vary from the imaginative and evocative use of language (for instance Sheldon and Blythe's *The Whale's Song*) to the figurative language of *Tigerella* (Wright) and the speech patterns of *Captain Abdul's Pirate School* (McNaughton).

Often what holds our attention in a good picture book may not be the length of the story or the complexity of the plot, but the enjoyment we derive from the shades of meaning. In fact, the length of most picture books is an advantage here, because they are not too time-consuming to reread.

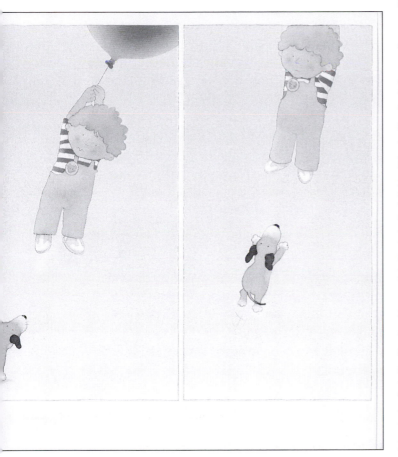

by permission of Hodder and Stoughton Limited

What can they teach us?

It would be difficult to list all that we can learn from picture books because any list would be as varied as the books we used. Like all good stories, picture books are part of the process of reflecting on life and those who live it, helping us to understand and celebrate the diversity of human experience. However, there do seem to be some common areas in which these books have a key role to play.

Firstly, they introduce us to narrative in picture and written text. By building on children's existing experience of story, picture books can teach us how stories work. So, for instance, Allan and Janet Ahlberg's *It Was a Dark and Stormy Night* provides a humorous insight into the relationship between author, narrator and character as the main character begins to hijack the story. And such devices as the retelling of traditional stories (for example, Jon Scieszka and Steve Johnson's *The Frog Prince Continued* or *The Three Little Wolves and the Big Bad Pig* by Eugene Trivizas and Helen Oxenbury) show us how we relate one story to another.

Secondly, picture books introduce us to different kinds of texts in interesting ways. The letter form propels the narrative of Simon James's *Dear Greenpeace*, whereas Babbette Cole's *Dr Dog* contains a subtle interplay between narrative and information writing. Other authors and illustrators draw on conventions from different traditions, such as the children's comic (for example, Colin McNaughton) or the use of visual symbolism in the work of Anthony Browne.

Thirdly, picture books can teach us about ourselves and about others in our culturally diverse society. The visual dimension of the picture book can be a particularly powerful way to present positive images of minority groups (see Merchant 1992). So books like *Handa's Surprise* (Eileen Browne) and *Masai and I* (Virginia Kroll) have a particularly important role to play, not simply because they offer positive images, but also because they are carefully constructed picture books. The picture book can also introduce us to the complexities of contemporary life. For the older reader, a book like *Always Adam* (Sheldon Oberman and Ted Lewin) offers us insights into the dynamics of ethnic and religious identity through the story of migration and changing traditions. Not only does it develop a sense of empathy, it also leaves us with unanswered questions about continuity and tradition and the development of new identities.

Finally, the visual element of the picture book helps us towards a closer and more critical reading of images. Illustration may also provide support in visualising the story. And so it could be argued that the visual representation of character and setting is helping young readers to see the story: in a sense they are 'scaffolding' the imagination.

Reading a picture book, just like reading any other work of fiction, is sooner or later to do with responding to the whole text and bringing meaning to it. It is about gaining information and enjoyment; about raising questions as well as answering them. Good picture books, like all good books, teach us to think: 'they are machines that provoke further thought' (Eco 1989).

Is size important?

Picture books are now available in a variety of formats. Publishers have produced small versions of popular titles – as small as a pocket diary or notebook – as well as the standard-sized versions. It is interesting for children to compare different versions and different imprints of the same text. Some titles are also available as 'big books' for use as shared texts, perhaps as part of a Literacy Hour or a more informal book-sharing session. As teachers we need to understand when using a big book is appropriate and when it is not.

We would want to argue that the big book has a particular role to play in classroom work. The idea of using a large text has a tradition that predates the National Literacy Strategy. Holdaway's (1979) descriptions of teachers and children sharing enlarged texts show how this sort of interaction mirrors the sort of learning that happens in more informal contexts, such as when a parent shares a book with a child at home. The advantage of the big book is simply that print and illustration can be seen by all children in the class at the same time. There is no magic – it's sometimes just easier to share a book in this way. So using big books helps to establish a community of readers in the class – a community that can discuss and reflect upon a shared experience.

Big books also allow the teacher to model specific reading behaviours and to draw attention to those aspects of print and image that are important to the story. So, for instance, we may want to explore why the phrase 'some things change and some things don't' is repeated in *Always Adam* (Oberman and Lewin), and what effect this has; or why Martin Waddell depicts the farmer lying in bed eating chocolates in

Farmer Duck, and what this tells us about his character. These seem more beneficial uses of the big book, more central to the construction of meaning than counting the number of full stops on the page!

So we can see that a big book has certain practical advantages for certain kinds of teaching. However, it would be a shame if we were limited to using only those books that are available in big book format, or led to believe that the enlarged text is the only way to introduce picture books to children.

As we have seen, revisiting our favourite picture book is useful and enjoyable. If this book is available in a large format this may well be an advantage. But the temptation to approach the same text in the same way each day of the week must be avoided. It would be a shame if the rich benefits offered by high quality books were smothered by a dull routine.

Conclusion

In this chapter we have looked at how the picture book genre draws its strength from the rich interplay between verbal and visual information. We have argued that this makes these texts a particularly powerfully medium for learning and teaching. Children throughout their primary years can be encouraged to look carefully and critically at print and visual image in picture books.

We have seen how picture books can encourage active reading and active meaning-making. We have argued that this is most likely to be achieved in a situation where children are working with a skilled reader who can introduce them to ways of looking at and talking about their readings. In this way they can build the emotional and intellectual meanings that are an essential part of good reading.

Talking and thinking about text are key features of the most effective reading. Perhaps in the end it is where our reading takes us that is important. Proust observes that 'our own wisdom begins where that of the author leaves off' (Proust 1994, p. 30), and this is an aspect of reading that is sometimes curiously reduced by the use of the term 'response' in curriculum guidance and commentaries.

2 Making opportunities for reading picture books

When a story is read to children, the shape of the story is created, the characters emerge, and the style of discourse and the literary turn of phrase are 'heard'. As a consequence, prediction and anticipation become easier at a second hearing. When the language of books is read aloud, this introduces new language forms to the ear making them a little easier to listen to next time. Meanings can be negotiated in discussion before, during and after reading. Reading to children and allowing interaction provide opportunities for new learning about texts.

(Clay 1991, p. 264)

In this chapter we look at different ways of introducing children to picture books. We begin by drawing on the themes explored in the previous chapter, considering the kinds of understandings which we are aiming to develop through our use of these texts. We then focus on using picture books in the Literacy Hour by looking at shared reading, guided reading and independent reading. Reading with other children is also included in this section under 'Reading partners'. The chapter concludes with suggestions on how to develop this work outside the context of the Literacy Hour.

What kinds of understandings are we aiming to develop?

Introducing children to picture books is an introduction to the whole process of reading. Such an introduction can involve developing a sense of enjoyment of text as we make new meanings and enter into imaginary worlds and will help children to build their understanding of the purpose of reading. But it can also involve learning about how texts work, and how authors and illustrators make use of the choices available to them.

These two strands can be described in terms of *learning to make meaning* and *learning how texts work*. We suggest that these are not 'either/or' teaching decisions. Learning to make meaning will be achieved by good teachers doing what they have always done: choosing high quality books and sharing them with enthusiasm. Learning how texts work will partly be achieved through teachers' interpretation of the National Literacy Strategy and partly through structured discussion of children's reading and writing across the curriculum. Striking a balance between the two strands is important simply because learning to make meaning and enjoy texts enriches our understanding of how texts work and vice versa (Thomas 1998).

Learning to make meaning includes:

- developing interest, excitement and enjoyment of text;
- entering into the world of the story;
- sharing enjoyment and response with other children and adults;

- thinking about how stories relate to other stories and other kinds of texts;
- learning and making sense of our world;
- introducing us to other worlds – real and imagined;
- helping us to talk and think about, and reflect on, our experience.

Learning how texts work includes:

- looking at how print and image work together in picture books;
- discussing the work, themes and approaches of different authors and illustrators;
- understanding how to read images, viewpoints and visual style;
- talking about how print is used on the page (e.g. where line breaks and page breaks occur);
- examining genre and story structure;
- looking at the effect of the presentational features of print (e.g. font size and style);
- examining the language features of texts;
- exploring the effect of the grammatical choices;
- talking about the word-level features.

Shared reading

As we saw in the previous chapter, the concept of shared reading predates the National Literacy Strategy, and it is important to recognise that there are different ways of, and different reasons for, sharing text. So the original rationale for shared reading, which involved replicating the features of 'the bedtime story' in the classroom context (Holdaway 1979), is rather different from mechanically identifying the title and author of a big book each time it is read and reread. Holdaway's aims were to promote enjoyment and enthusiasm for reading by introducing children to the power of written language. Some interpretations of the National Literacy Strategy can limit the potential of shared reading by a rather rigid interpretation of teaching objectives.

In the Literacy Hour, shared reading normally takes place as a whole-class session during the first 15 minutes of the hour. However, there are other occasions when it is quite appropriate as a group activity (see Laycock 1999). Shared reading is based on the idea of the teacher modelling reading behaviour. In this sort of reading activity, the teacher 'scaffolds' children's learning. She will model the skills and strategies that are used in reading, while encouraging as much interaction as possible from the class or group. The approach is applicable to any age range and should have clear learning objectives which are relevant to the class or group. A shared reading session might, for instance, use a big book such as *Farmer Duck* by Martin Waddell to explore story structure in terms of situation–problem–solution–evaluation or it might use the same text to make inferences about what the animals are discussing in their secret meeting.

Shared reading can focus on different aspects of the reading process, including comprehension, organisational structure, presentational features or any of the objectives outlined in the text-level section of the National Literacy Strategy Framework for Teaching (DfEE, Department for Education and Employment, 1998). It is important not to choose too many learning objectives for a shared reading session. The text-level activities suggested in this book list possibilities for shared reading for you to choose from. It is not envisaged that you will use all the ideas.

The success of shared reading depends partly on the choice of text and partly on the teaching approach. While we are advised to choose texts that are pitched at a high enough level to 'stretch' the teaching group, we shall recall that one of the features of a good picture book is that it is multi-layered. So the texts used in this book invite a variety of readings and will involve and include children at different levels. They will not lose their appeal when we turn our attention from *learning to make meaning* to *learning how texts work* (Graham 1999).

A balanced approach to shared reading will include extended reading aloud from entire texts – without breaking off to comment on the narrative, to check on understanding or to elicit predictions. It will, at times, allow texts to 'speak for themselves' and will also allow children to respond in an open and unstructured way as they construct their own meanings and interpretations. Effective shared reading is based on an understanding that variety is important in cultivating and maintaining enthusiastic readers. Always approaching a text in the same way may not be helpful. Confident teachers are now looking at how discussion, shared writing or the use of a different text can be used as a prelude to a shared reading session.

Some shared reading of picture books will inevitably involve children and teachers in the close examination of visual elements such as the choice of images, the use of colour and the 'point of view'. This may involve quite close analysis (e.g. the visual style in *Snow White in New York* or the animal characteristics of the visitors in *Zoo*) and lead into discussion about the relationship between the visual and the verbal both in these texts and in the wider print environment.

Guided reading

Guided reading involves the teacher in closely supporting a group of readers who work individually from multiple copies of the same text. The learning objectives will be carefully matched to the children in the group. The teacher will look at text-, sentence- or word-level features of children's reading and provide quite explicit guidelines on the required task. So, for example, in reading the story of *Handa's Surprise* by Eileen Browne the teacher may focus on the children's use of picture cues to support meaning and may explicitly refer to techniques such as phonic analysis and self-correction in introducing the session. Older pupils will be involved in exploring and analysing texts. In a guided read of *Snow White in New York* they may be looking closely at visual and verbal elements of the text to see the relationship between the characters is represented through their positioning on the page, the use of colour, style of speech and punctuation. After this initial orientation, children will then work through the task at their own rate while the teacher provides individual guidance and support, keeping a careful record of children's performance.

Picture books are important resources to use in guided reading and provide children with the opportunity to apply the skills and strategies that they have learnt in shared reading on texts that are carefully matched to their reading ability.

Independent reading

Independent reading requires children to work without the help of the teacher. Here, the reading skills and strategies learnt through shared and guided work can be brought together. Again, picture books from a selection of 'core texts' are a useful resource for this sort of reading (see Ellis and Barrs 1996). Children can be encouraged to choose reading material from a 'core text' selection made up of books that they are already familiar with from an earlier shared or guided reading session. Because of their particular characteristics, picture books lend themselves readily to this sort of re-reading. Even quite confident older readers will benefit by rereading the books they enjoyed when they were younger. It is certainly worth making these picture books available to older readers.

While there is a limited amount of time available for independent reading in the Literacy Hour, the National Literacy Strategy Framework for Teaching encourages us to develop this practice elsewhere in the school day (DfEE 1998, p. 14). This is an important message, since we do not want to give beginning readers the idea that reading is limited to a particular time of day, or area of the classroom. The same is true for more experienced readers who will also need to become accustomed to the rewards and routines of more sustained extended reading.

Reading partners

Pairing older children with younger children as reading partners has become a popular practice in many schools. Not only does it help to raise the profile of reading, but it can also provide a non-threatening context for sharing and talking about books – and this can work for both sides of the partnership. For example, older readers may gain insight into their own reading strategies, they may learn more about the subtleties of the picture book form and their own confidence and motivation will increase.

Of course, a system of reading partnerships needs to be carefully organised. While arrangements between two classes in a school can be quite effective, a whole-school approach is preferable. Older children will need some simple guidance on building relationships and techniques for sharing while younger children will also need to be carefully prepared. (For further guidance on setting up reading partnerships refer to Graham and Kelly 1997.)

Taking it further

While using picture books will form a natural part of work in the Literacy Hour, there will be plenty of other opportunities for developing children's interest in these texts. In this section we explore some possibilities. First and foremost it will be important to protect story time as an occasion in which these books can be enjoyed in their own right. In story time exclusive attention is paid to learning to make meaning and enjoying reading. The National Literacy Strategy Framework for Teaching suggests that additional time may be needed for 'continuing the practice of reading to the class' (DfEE 1998, p. 14), and we should make the most of this throughout the primary years.

Although story time is often used as a way of drawing a class together at the end of the school day, this may not necessarily be the best occasion for children to enjoy or respond to a good story. As Thomas comments:

> Story time isn't a filler between afternoon break and home time. It should be an essential part of a child's introduction to reading . . . Story time provides the opportunity to introduce children to texts in which the demands made on the reader are matched by the rewards of the text. (Thomas 1998, p. 148)

There will also be times when it is appropriate to encourage a more open-ended response to books you have shared. Here, children can be encouraged to reflect in a variety of ways on what they have read or heard. This reflection might involve discussion, close investigation of texts, writing or recording a response more graphically.

If we believe in the educational value of shared narrative then we will be using picture books in our teaching in a variety of ways and at different times during the school day. As well as simply enjoying this reading we shall be able to make natural links with other areas of the curriculum. We have suggested such links in the material we have chosen and show that some picture books lend themselves to teaching about social, cultural and religious issues, while others lead us into curriculum subjects such as history or mathematics. Some picture books, of course, can be used as vehicles to explore the wider English curriculum through drama and role-play, poetry or the study of different kinds of texts.

From time to time it is important to raise the profile of reading in the classroom. Focusing on an author of the week or a book of the week is one approach that can be used. This is a useful focus for display work and can also help to inform colleagues and parents of the work being undertaken. Most publishers can provide additional information about authors and illustrators if given sufficient warning. You can also make a collection of 'authorgraphs' from the magazine *Books for Keeps* or by Internet searches. (Further information sources are listed under useful addresses at the end of this book.)

It may also be useful to raise the profile of picture books in the school as a whole. Clearly you would need to engage the support of the English coordinator, the head teacher and other teaching staff to do this. Whole-school events such as book weeks can be organised and might include visits by authors, a school bookshop, story trails or dressing up as characters from books. (A fuller treatment of whole-school events is given in Merchant and Marsh 1998.)

As we saw in the previous chapter, picture books can be used to develop interesting work with parents. Often teachers report that parents tend to see reading in terms of a race in which fewer pictures, smaller print and thicker books are an indication of progress. This is not surprising if we consider the ways in which progress in reading is presented. Political rhetoric about raising standards, meeting targets and increasing levels of attainment often sit rather uncomfortably with messages about sharing and enjoying what you read. The idea of reading as a race is unfortunately reinforced by some reading schemes which encourage the view that there are simple measures of progress in reading.

Involving parents in story-sharing workshops is one way of encouraging their interest and building a familiarity with picture books. This will provide you with an opportunity to communicate some important attitudes to reading and allay anxieties around progress in reading. Recent work on story packs with young children focuses on developing talk and play at home, based on the themes in a book. A pack based on *Farmer Duck* might include the following (from Merchant and Marsh 1998):

- an audio tape of the story;
- a toy duck;
- toy animals (e.g. cows, sheep and hens);
- finger puppets of some of the animals and the farmer;
- a board game based on the story;
- a crossword containing key words from the book;
- a quiz about the book;
- an information book or video about farms and farming;
- a farm jigsaw;
- poems and nursery rhymes about farm animals;
- snap/lotto games based on the book.

These sorts of ideas can be extended and developed for different age groups, providing a useful support for purposeful work around picture books in the home environment.

Conclusion

In this chapter we have looked at the place of picture books in the primary classroom. We have drawn attention to the role that they can play in the various component parts of the Literacy Hour because we recognise that this will be the focus of attention for many teacher colleagues. However, we have also pointed out how picture books can be used at other times in the school day and for other purposes. At the end of Chapter 1 we drew attention to the importance of talking and thinking about text, and this theme is picked up as we see how picture books forge links with other subject areas and offer us ways into cross-curricular issues.

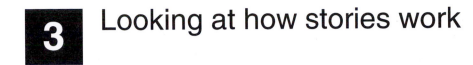

3 Looking at how stories work

Pleasure in a literary book comes from discovering the pattern of event, of character, of ideas, of image of language woven into it. Books for very young children are designed in pictures and words that allow this discovery to take place…When they have enjoyed this experience a number of times they gradually learn what time and effort they must give in order to receive the return pleasure that makes reading worthwhile.'

(Chambers 1991, p. 12)

In this chapter we turn our attention to picture books that we have found particularly useful for teaching about how stories work. Although any narrative can be used for developing this sort of understanding, the picture books we focus on have offered particularly useful ways into the exploration of story structure and story elements such as character, plot and setting, as some of the photocopiable activities illustrate.

These picture books have been used to explore the themes of:

- story structure – situation, problem, solution and evaluation;
- chronology – the sequence of events and the treatment of time;
- characterisation – in both visual and print features;
- narrative voice and viewpoint – who is telling the story and whose point of view the illustration represents;
- intertextuality – how stories relate to one another (including texts in other media).

The titles in this chapter

Anthony Browne	*Voices in the Park*
Fiona French	*Snow White in New York*
Janet & Allan Ahlberg	*It Was a Dark and Stormy Night*
Colin McNaughton	*Have You Seen Who's Just Moved in Next Door to Us?*
Madhur Jaffrey	*Seasons of Splendour*
Marcia Williams	*Mr William Shakespeare's Plays*

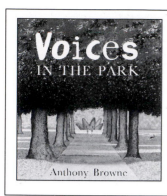

Voices in the park

Written and illustrated by Anthony Browne.

Doubleday ISBN 0-385-408587
© 1998 by A.E.T. Browne and Partners. Designed by Ian Butterworth. Published by Doubleday, a division of Transworld Publishers, a division of The Random House Group Ltd.

Learning opportunities

Range: stories with familiar settings; stories that raise issues; texts with language play.

Themes: point of view; the way different characters respond to different characters and events, stories told from a range of perspectives.

Terminology: point of view; narrator; character.

Outline

Two parents, one quite wealthy and the other a gentle unemployed father, and their children on a visit to the local park. The story of their visit is told four times. Each time the same events are narrated from a different point of view. These differences are reflected in the ways the four narratives are illustrated.

Ways of working

Text

Four voices

Children can read the four stories and, in each separate narrative, focus on the voice of the narrator. Their aim should be to form a general impression of this narrator – what they are like, what they think about things and how they feel. They could try reading the text and vocalising the way they think these characters talk. As a way into the story they could make notes about each narrator in four columns, side by side. Comparing these can show some of the differences between the characters in the story.

Feelings and illustrations

The way each character feels should be looked at through further reading of the story. Once they realise the way the book is structured children find it interesting to contrast the way the four characters feel about their lives and the walk in the park. One vital element of this is the way in which the illustrations are different for each narrative. There is the brilliant comparison of the walk to and from the park in the unemployed dad's narrative, in which surreal additions to the illustration reflect his mood. Each narrative adopts a different level of colour, with the little girl having the brightest pictures. The skies are different, ranging from grim to clear blue. And yet all these variations occur in scenes of a narrative that happened under the same sky and in the same park. This is particularly effective in scenes where the same event, such as the two children meeting on the park bench, is illustrated in different ways. The effect of this contrast can be to further extend children's thoughts about how the illustrations reflect the feelings of the characters.

Point of view

The four narratives provide an excellent example of narration being communicated from a particular point of view. This is a feature of all narratives: the way the narrator feels about things will come out in the language used and the way scenes are described. The children can compare the different points of view by making a list of all the events that took place during the visit to the park. Some, like the children's turns on the slide, only appear in one of the four narratives. Once they have made a full list of things that happened during the visit they can note alongside the way different characters describe it. For example, they can look at the way the two children and the mother describe the point at which she calls her son to go home.

Another view

Children can be encouraged to express their own points of view in response to the narratives. One way of doing this is to ask them to produce a fifth story to run alongside the others. They could imagine themselves as the fifth character at the park watching all this happen. How would they have seen it? How would they have reacted to the different characters?

Sentence

Same thing; different words

Through the four narratives different words are used to describe the same thing. For example, the mother describes the girl as 'a very rough-looking child', whereas the boy describes her as 'quite nice'. Children can look at the different descriptions produced by the four characters.

Font

The four separate narratives are printed in different fonts. Children can look at these and try explaining how each font could reflect the voice of the narrator.

Why, for example, is the little boy's story told in such thin, faint type?

Word notes

As a set of first person narratives the text gives a good opportunity for you to look at the '-ed' ending of verbs. Children can try putting the past tense verbs into their base form and looking at the spelling rules that come into play as words are switched from present to past tense and vice versa.

Extension

Perspective drawing

As a further development of the idea of point of view children can work in groups drawing the same thing, such as an arrangement of 3D shapes or a set of objects, from varied points of view. They can compare the way in which their differing perspectives lead to varied end results.

Historical viewpoints

Within the history curriculum there are opportunities to look at how different narrators recounted historical events from various perspectives and the ways in which this coloured their telling. The Fall of Troy, the conditions of the Victorian poor and beheading of Mary, Queen of Scots – all present opportunities for looking at the way in which different voices narrated the same event.

Links to other texts

Voices in the Park is a reworking of Anthony Browne's *A Walk in the Park*.

Children could also look at *The Visitors Who Came to Stay* by Annalena McAffee and Anthony Browne, and *Changes* by Browne. Both provide examples of the ways in which the illustrations reflect the feelings of characters.

DESCRIBING THE VOICES

Choose the best adjectives to describe each of the 'voices' in the story *Voices in the Park*.

Adjectives			
young	happy	shy	friendly	posh
quiet	upset	hard	timid	
miserable	nasty	sensitive	harsh	gritty
tired				
weary	bold	caring	sad	hopeful	soft

First voice	**Second voice**	Third voice	Fourth *voice*

Can you add any more adjectives?

THE VOICES SAY . . .

How would the four voices react to different things? What would they say about . . .

a rollercoaster?

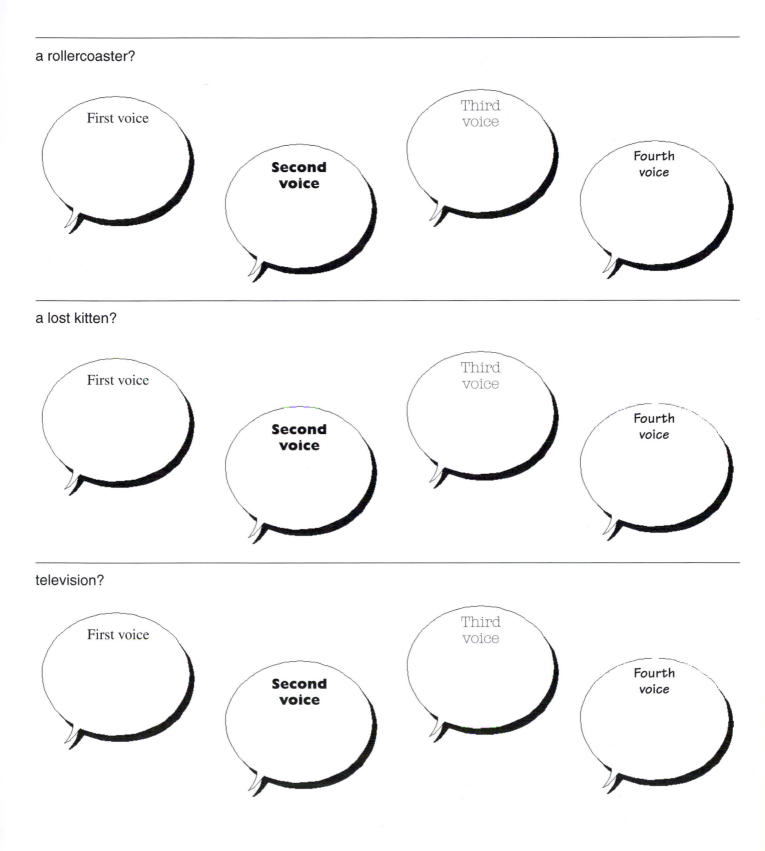

a lost kitten?

television?

Snow White in New York

Written and illustrated by Fiona French.

Oxford University Press ISBN 0-192-72210-7

Learning opportunities

Range: traditional stories retold; texts with language play.

Themes: exploring characters; good triumphing over evil; visual media.

Terminology: story structure; chronological sequence; setting; character; plot development.

Outline

The traditional European story is retold in the New York of the 1920s. Snow White's stepmother is surrounded by shadowy figures clutching violin cases as she plots to do away with 'the Belle of New York City'. Snow White escapes, securing a job as a singer in a jazz club, where she falls in love with a newspaper reporter. Later, her stepmother manages to slip a poisoned cherry in Snow White's cocktail and she dies. New York mourns her death and the funeral takes place in the pouring rain – but there is a 'surprise' happy ending!

Ways of working

Text

Plot structure
After the first reading of *Snow White in New York*, ask children to list the similarities and differences between this and the traditional story. Collect several copies of the traditional version first. Ask children to create a time line, charting events, to compare the versions. Look at how the scene is set in the different versions. Then look at how the 'problem' of rivalry and jealousy is set up, how tension is built up through the step-mother's actions and how events are resolved as good triumphs over evil.

Story elements
Through comparing versions you can also draw attention to specific story elements. Compare *where* the events take place, *how* they are depicted in verbal and visual elements, *how* the characters are created and *what* happens. Make sure children focus on both similarities and differences. Extend this by asking them to draft a version of the story that takes place in a different context (e.g. the immediate locality or a future 'Star Trek' science-fiction setting).

Looking at the illustrations
Fiona French gives the Snow White story a new setting by combining the features of a specific visual style with elements of Hollywood gangster films. Ask children to work in groups and look at the illustrations. Sketches of specific images can be accompanied by notes on what effect they have. Model this by looking at the cover – the dress style of Snow White, the towering skyscrapers, the sun like a spotlight and the use of lines that evoke the design style of the era. This can lead

into a discussion of stereotypes as you compare the blonde-haired blue-eyed Snow White with her stepmother, or the gangsters and the reporter.

Sentence

Despite the complexities of this re-telling, Fiona French is economical in her use of language and this seems to evoke the 'staccato' effect of narration in the gangster genre. Simple sentences are used to create this effect (e.g. 'She was alive.'; 'She went inside.') – this can lead into a discussion of simple and complex sentences. Ask children to think about contraction in sentences. The title is a good starting point: what would be the effect of retitling the book *The Exciting Adventures of Snow White in New York*? Ask children to look at the newspaper headlines and hoardings in the book that also involve contraction.

Extension

- Turn key events in the story into newspaper reports (using the headlines in the book as starting points).

Word notes

Look at the language features that help us to place this story in America. On the photocopiable we have referred to these as 'Americanisms', but you can also talk about slang and idiomatic speech. For example, the stepmother talks about 'getting rid' of Snow White – how many other expressions can children think of as alternatives (e.g. 'doing away with'; 'disposing of', etc.). Discuss the effect of using these expressions.

- Write newspaper headlines for other traditional stories or rhymes (e.g. 'Wolf posed as grandmother'; 'Poor diet blamed on troll'; 'Duke's military manoeuvres "futile"').
- Rewrite another traditional tale in a new setting (e.g. Red Riding Hood in London), thinking about how the characters, events and illustrations could be adapted. Children could also consider the use of appropriate language features or slang.
- Compare *Snow White in New York* with other books by Fiona French (e.g. *Anancy and Mr Drybone*).

Links to other texts

Older children will enjoy looking at earlier versions of the Snow White story. A collection of Grimm's Tales would be useful here – particularly those from the teacher's own childhood. This could lead to some interesting work in looking at the changes in children's literature. With a little research you can find the story in German – you don't need a knowledge of the language to study illustration or guess the meaning of 'Spieglein, Spieglein an der Wand, wer ist die Schönste im Land?'

Snow White in New York is part of a growing collection of stories that rework traditional tales. Some other examples are *The Three Little Wolves and the Big Bad Pig* (Trivizas and Oxenbury), *Prince Cinders* (Cole) and the stories of Jon Scieszka, which include *The True Story of the Three Little Pigs*, *The Frog Prince Continued* and *The Stinky Cheese Man and Other Fairly Stupid Tales*. In the same vein you could also read Roald Dahl's *Revolting Rhymes*.

SORT THEM OUT – AND MAKE IT SNAPPY!

Snow White in New York uses a lot of Americanisms. Find the Americanisms used in the book.

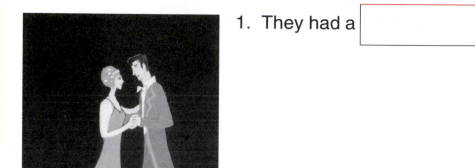

1. They had a [   ] wedding.

2. Once upon a time in New York there was a [   ] called Snow White.

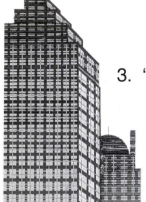

3. 'Take her [   ] and shoot her,' she said to one of her bodyguards.

4. All the papers said that Snow White's stepmother was the [   ] in New York.

But one day she read something that made her very jealous.

5. Snow White [   ] of New York city.

SNOW WHITE IN NEW YORK: THE CHARACTERS

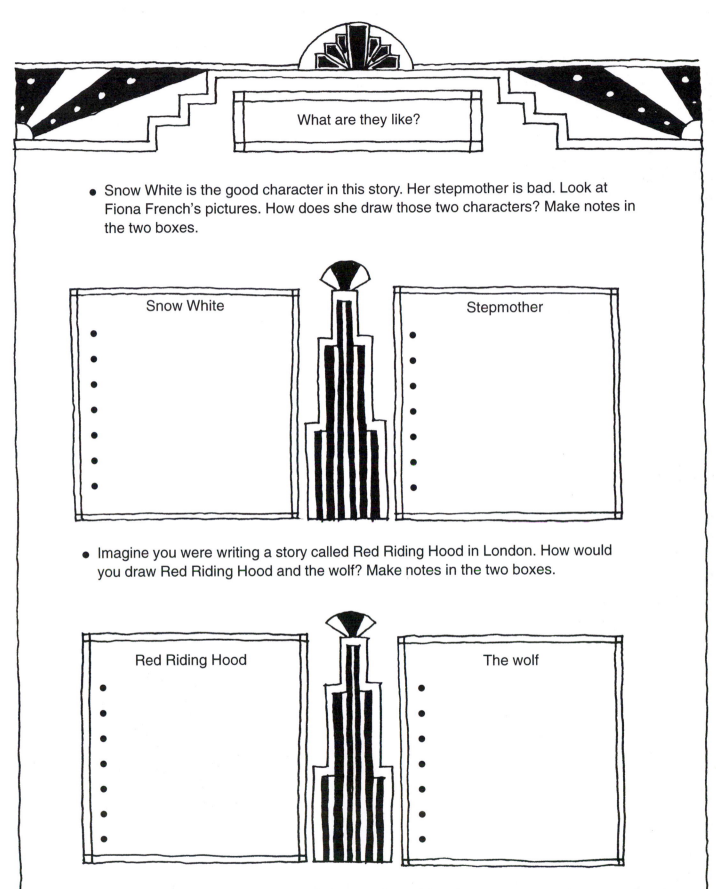

What are they like?

- Snow White is the good character in this story. Her stepmother is bad. Look at Fiona French's pictures. How does she draw those two characters? Make notes in the two boxes.

Snow White
-
-
-
-
-
-
-

Stepmother
-
-
-
-
-
-

- Imagine you were writing a story called Red Riding Hood in London. How would you draw Red Riding Hood and the wolf? Make notes in the two boxes.

Red Riding Hood
-
-
-
-
-
-
-

The wolf
-
-
-
-
-
-

- Plan your version of this Story on the other side of the sheet.

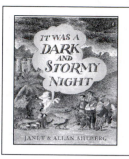

It Was a Dark and Stormy Night

Written by Allan Ahlberg and illustrated by Janet Ahlberg

Puffin ISBN 0-140-54586-7

Learning opportunities

Range: stories about imagined worlds; fantasy adventure; traditional stories.

Themes: essential story ingredients; oral storytelling; narration.

Terminology: story structure; opening/setting; comparison of adjectives.

Outline

Antonio, 'a small, brave, eight-year-old boy', is captured by a band of brigands and taken from the valley, where he lives with his family, into the mountains. To amuse the brigands, he is asked by their chief to make up a story to pass the time (Scheherazade-like). This Antonio does with great skill, drawing on the conventional ingredients of adventure stories. His ever-increasingly complex story lines eventually provide him with an ingenious method of escape.

Ways of working

Text

Creating varieties of story
The text itself is very inventive in offering different ways of telling stories. Firstly, focus on the different ways of creating a setting. Compare and contrast with the children the examples that Antonio actually provides: 'It was a dark and stormy night'; 'It was a cold and frosty night'. Make a list of the type of setting where a story can take place. Keep it general (e.g. 'a magic land' rather than 'Narnia'). Look at these various setting types from stories and compile adjectives that describe them. Use these in the creation of new story settings.

Retelling the story
Once the children are familiar with the story, they can be encouraged to think about how Antonio might have started to tell it to the Panetta family, as indicated at the end: 'and began his story'. Using the first page of the text, explore with the children alternative beginnings which begin with 'It was a dark and stormy night' but include the story of Antonio's own kidnapping, which the family would also want to know.

Producing a cartoon magazine
Spend some time looking at how cartoon strips work in terms of picture, speech and text. Using the illustrations and dialogue from *It Was a Dark and Stormy Night* (e.g. the banquet scene), get the children to construct a comic version of some of the events. This will involve separating a section of the story into frames and transposing the dialogue into speech bubbles.

Oral storytelling
Have storytelling sessions beginning with the 'it was a dark and stormy night' opening. Sit the children in a circle and have one child add a line to the opening then continue to build a story around the group. This can be varied by introducing different elements at appropriate stages

(e.g. another character is introduced; the setting is changed; something happens, etc.)

Sentence

Look at some of the different environments described in the text, e.g. the 'high and handsome castle'. Look at the descriptions of these (e.g. 'There were mysterious clankings in the dungeons'; 'headless people on the battlements' etc.). Encourage the children to extend the accounts in different ways, e.g. 'creaking floorboards in the attic'. Make a list of some of the interesting and varied adjectives used to enhance the settings in the story.

Find drawings and pictures from other sources which might provide useful settings for adventure stories and build up similar sets of descriptions, drawing on the list of adjectives and others the class contribute.

Word notes

Much is made of the potential 'compound' elements of meanings of words that are not normally viewed in this way. e.g. kid-napping (stealing young goats). Use some of these examples to show children how compound words are constructed. Highlight other words from the text and play with their potential meaning, e.g. brig-ands; tooth-brush; cut-lasses; mega-phone. For example, an 'am-bush' could be a 'bush' in which I 'am' hiding.

Extension

- Play the Alternatives Game along the lines suggested in the text, e.g. Fabrizzi hurled the gorgonzola at the chief and (1) missed *or* (2) hit him in the eye.

    Create possibilities for other parts of the story, where two events could have happened and ask the children to make notes on how the story could have developed if it had taken an alternative route.

- Play the Rhyme Game along the lines suggested in the story. The children are given one sentence (e.g. 'The awful Thingy left its watery lair') and are asked to create a following rhyming sentence (e.g. 'And came out dripping up the stair').

- Using the items of food listed for the banquet, create appropriate menus to describe what is being prepared in different styles, e.g. contrast restaurant with roadside café. To do this effectively you will need to look at some original menu formats, so that you can take an item from text (e.g. roast potatoes) and create a 'roadside cafe' version – Roast Pots. – and a restaurant version: Pommes Rotis.

- Using the references to the Thingy in the text as a source, create a news reporter's account (for radio or television) from the scene. This might include interviews with appropriate people, similar to a report on the Loch Ness Monster. An alternative format would be an article in a newspaper; use an appropriate computer program to achieve relevant formats.

- Look carefully at the English/Italian examples of food on the brigands' menu. Research popular foods from a range of countries and construct appropriate examples from the following countries: Spain, India, Denmark. Compare and contrast any characteristic spelling patterns.

Links to Other Texts

Read *Three by the Sea* by Edward and James Marshall. This text similarly allows you to discuss with children what makes a 'good story'. It also has a splendid example of the characters involved in the storytelling becoming involved in their own story structure (just like the brigands)!

SETTING WORDS

Think of a setting for a story,

e.g.:

Setting	
castle	

Describe *who* is there.

Describe *what* they are like.

Describe *where* they are in the location.

POSSIBLE SETTINGS

castle

rainforest

spaceship

spooky house

underground cave

pirate ship

Wild West town

e.g.:

Setting	Who is there?	What are they like?	Where are they?
castle	prisoners	starving	in the dungeon

Fill in this setting words chart:

Setting	Who is there?	What are they like?	Where are they?

Book cover and illustration (p.11) from IT WAS A DARK AND STORMY NIGHT by Janet and Allan Ahlberg (Viking, 1993). Text and illustrations copyright © Janet and Allan Ahlberg, 1993. Reproduced by permission of Penguin Books Ltd.

IT WAS A . . .

Find adjectives to fit the spaces below, making your own 'It was a . . .' story openings. You could use words from the adjectives bin – *but only use each of them once.*

It was a _____ and _____ day.

It was a _____ and _____ forest.

It was a _____ and _____ bridge.

It was a _____ and _____ house.

It was a _____ and _____ dragon.

It was a _____ and _____ pool.

It was a _____ and _____ spider.

It was a _____ and _____ cliff.

Adjective bin

vicious   cool   venomous   bright   steep   high   rainy

dense

hairy   rickety   derelict   cold   scary

tall   horrible   spooky   clear   sunny   dull

scaly   deep   fiery   tangled   treacherous

Have You Seen Who's Just Moved in Next Door to Us?

Written and illustrated by Colin McNaughton.

Walker Books ISBN 0-744-53043-1

Learning opportunities

Range: stories with familiar settings; poems based on observation; traditional stories; a range of text types.

Themes: characters and story plot.

Terminology: story structure; rhyme; homophone; poetic forms.

Outline

The reader is gradually introduced to some 'strange' inhabitants of a block of terraced houses, who are all worried about the recent arrival of some new neighbours. There is much talk of who they are, and as this happens we are introduced to some well-known characters, including Burglar Bill, King Kong and Superman, alongside aliens, ghosts, bikers and pirates.

Ways of working

Text

Researching 'original' stories and well-known people

The text introduces the reader to characters from several well-known tales (both classic and nursery). Plot, with the children, the characters, settings and main events in the original stories (e.g. character: Humpty Dumpty; setting: sitting on a wall; main event: fell off and injured himself). This activity will familiarise the children with the main characters and plot elements in the stories. Ask children to select a set number of characters from the text and provide this sort of profile on each of them. In terms of 'well-known' people (e.g. Michelangelo) an investigation could be set up to explore who they were and what they did.

Misheard whispers

As the news of 'new neighbours' passes down the street it is misheard. It becomes 'nude neighbours' and then 'rude wavers'. Children can collect the list of misheard whispers as they pass along the rows and look at how the message alters.

Producing similar picture texts

Based on nursery rhymes (Little Bo-Peep), fairy tales (Cinderella), other books (*The Very Hungry Caterpillar*) and famous people (Pharohs from *The Egyptian News*), children could be encouraged to create their own 'house texts'. Prepare a container with slips of paper on which the names of people who live in a particular house are written. Ask the children to randomly select one from the container, then research the original and, on this basis, create a suitable 'house' with appropriate characters and dialogue. They could devise a couplet modelled on the original text for this character and concluding with the sentence: 'Has — seen who's just moved in/Next door to us?'

Cut-away wall

In a similar style to the cut-away walls in the text, children can devise a house for a set of characters and show a cross-section of it. They can feature characters from a well-known story within this, adding speech bubbles in a style similar to the original. Point out that each house develops one clear joke, such as the 'egg-' words in the Dumpty's or the school teaching rude words. Groups of children can make their completed houses into a long, zigzag books.

Exploring characters

When the new neighbours are finally revealed at the end of the book, each inhabitant speaks (in character) against them: the dinosaur says 'monstrous'; the pirates say 'shiver me timbers'. Get the children to suggest appropriate comments for their own researched characters (e.g. Little Bo-Peep would say 'They look a bit sheepish'; Pharoah would dismiss them as 'Commoners'). Looking at the full list of characters in your street, ask the children to suggest various final declarations that could be made by other characters.

Sentence

Using a selection of comics, brainstorm a list of the kinds of dialogue that occur in strip cartoons: 'It's m-making my j-jaws shrink!'; 'Wahey! A flood!'; 'Pesky huskies ain't strong enough to pull ma sledge', etc. List some of the important features of this dialogue under headings: abbreviations/contractions (he'll, I'm, etc.); words for sounds ('SNARL!', 'puff!', etc.); spellings for effects ('m-making'; 'j-jaws'); dialect/ accent ('ain't', 'ma', etc.). Use some of the features isolated to create a selection of sayings for your own comic strip characters, e.g. Aladdin, Three Blind Mice, Snow White, etc.

Extension

- There is a cat on every page which moves you along the street. In front of different houses the cat is doing different things (walking on the roof, looking in a dustbin, etc. Create another animal (e.g. dog, mouse, etc.) and suggest activities for them related to the illustrations on each page.
- Collect a list of the shop names in the text. Look at appropriate shop/house names in the street the children have

Word Notes

In the book, look at the ways in which words/phrases are misheard as we progress down the street: 'new neighbours'; 'nude neighbours'; 'rude wavers'; 'blue quavers'; 'pooh savers'; 'shoe savers'; 'few favours'; 'chew sabres'; 'new neighbours'. Using a rhyming dictionary and a thesaurus, get the children to create their own misheard whispers based on other characters, e.g. Jack to the Giant: 'gold eggs'; 'old pegs'; 'cold legs'; etc. (With this activity it is best to choose combinations which offer lots of potential and few embarrassments!) This activity could be developed to look at the use of homophones (words that sound the same but have a different meaning) in *Have You Seen Who's Just Moved in Next Door to Us* (e.g. workers in Frankenstein's laboratory say: 'Would you like a hand, Mabel' and work in a 'body shop').

created. Collect examples of unusual shop names from other sources (e.g. local environment, town centre, etc.). The phone book can be an interesting resource for these – there is a tendency to get interesting puns in the names of hairdressers and chip shops.

- Ask the children to come up with sets into which they could sort the characters in the book. These could be 'goodies' and 'baddies'. They could go for 'old stories' and 'new stories'. Once they have devised two sets, ask them to sort a selection of characters in the story, then try the same activity with different sorting criteria.
- Children could try the cut-away wall activity with houses that are not opened in the text, such as Merlin's or Mr Muscle's. They have to think what it would look like inside this house.

WORD WHISPERS

Devise a whisper, just like in the book *Have You Seen Who's Just Moved in Next Door to Us?*
In that book 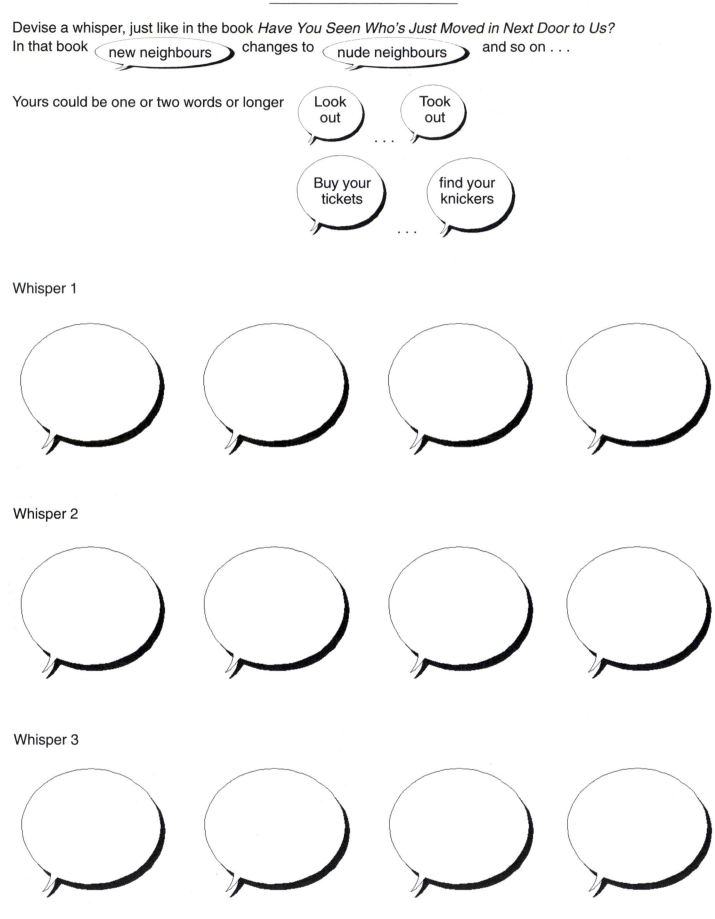 new neighbours changes to nude neighbours and so on . . .

Yours could be one or two words or longer

> Look out
>
> Took out
>
> . . .
>
> Buy your tickets
>
> find your knickers
>
> . . .

Whisper 1

Whisper 2

Whisper 3

STREET HUNT

Look through *Have You Seen Who's Just Moved in Next Door to Us?*

Find examples of the following . . .

Sound words

words for sounds
e.g. squelch

Homophones and puns

words with two
meanings or that sound
like other words
e.g. eggstra

Exclamations

words characters exclaim
e.g. UG!

Rude words

words to hide from your
teacher
e.g. Bum!

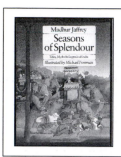

Seasons of Splendour

Written by Madhur Jaffrey and illustrated by Michael Foreman.

Pavilion Books ISBN 1-857-93364

Learning opportunities

Range: traditional stories; myths; legends; stories and poems from other cultures.

Themes: exploring characters; good triumphing over evil.

Terminology: story structure; setting; character; plot development.

Outline

Madhur Jaffrey offers her own versions of traditional tales from India. The stories are arranged in chronological order, from the May and June of one year to the March and April of the next, and contain a variety of tales, where gods and goddesses meet farmers, animal gods battle with evil demons for the good of mankind, and kings and queens show signs of human frailty. Jaffrey recommends that these tales should be read out aloud, and, for this purpose, there is a pronunciation section at the back of the book.

Ways of working

Text

Focus on story structure
Select any one of the stories and focus on its main events. Read the story to the children and get them to select what they consider to be the two main events of the story. For example, the story 'Lakshmi and the clever washerwoman' tends to highlight two important events: (1) the theft of the necklace, and (2) the dismissal of Poverty – highlighting the beginning (problem) and end (solution) of the story. This can lead to a discussion with the children about the main highlights of the story, and what it is that they consider to be the essential features. Once they have tried this activity with a range of stories children can look for similarities in the type of problems the characters face and the solutions that emerge.

Exploring character
Using the photocopiable, get the children to focus on the main characters in any one story. For example, in 'Lakshmi and the clever washerwoman', initially highlight all the words in the text that help to describe the characters of the King and the Queen. Then use the bottom sections of the chart to list words that are not in the text, but help to identify what they feel are the characteristics of these two. These could then be transferred to a larger chart, containing a drawing on the character; words highlighted drawn from the actual text in one colour and additional words highlighted that were suggested in red. This would enable children to explore literal/inferential skills in relation to the interpretation of character.

Exploring background
Focus on Madhur Jaffrey's introductions to each story to predict what the story might be about and also to explore the links between cultures. For example, again using 'Lakshmi and the clever washerwoman', it is possible to discuss (1) a story about pleasing the goddess, Lakshmi, and (2) the significance of

fireworks, lights and house-cleaning in the contexts of different cultures. As they do this, children will also build up a picture of Madhur Jaffrey as a narrator. Build up a profile of the narrator, listing things the children learn about her as they read the stories.

Pictorial representation.
Look at Michael Foreman's illustrations of each story. In particular, concentrate on what each picture tells about the story (i.e. in terms of events, characters, feelings): for example, in terms of 'Lakshmi and the clever washerwoman', the Queen is isolated from her helpers; she is relatively small, whereas the crow is large and threatening. What has he chosen to highlight in each story? Ask the children to select four pictures and, for each of them, list what is depicted in the illustration, describing what the various features look like. What expression do they have? What action are they performing? Can they find two illustrations that are similar? Can they find two that are very different?

Sentence

In any of the stories, a focus might well be on the paragraphing of the sentences. Explain to the children that a paragraph is a chunk of text focussing on one idea. Looking at a selected story, ask the children to count the number of paragraphs. Ask them to work with a partner, making a list that summarises the main things that occur in each paragraph.

Extension

- Write a diary entry of personal events related to community celebrations (e.g. spring cleaning, Bonfire Night, Chinese New Year, Christmas, Eid). Point out to children that they need to relate some of the details of these celebrations, explaining some of the various customs. In some cases this could involve interviewing members

Word notes

Collect examples of 'familiar' and 'unfamiliar' words from each story, for example, 'The birth of Krishna': 'wicked' (familiar); 'sprawled' (unfamiliar); 'sweet' (familiar); 'intervened' (unfamiliar). Look up both the meanings and the origins of these words. Consider their specific meaning in the text, as well as their other meanings in other contexts. For example, what is the meaning of the word 'sweet' in the context of 'sweet, gentle girl', and how does this relate to other dictionary meanings (fresh, pleasant, etc.)?

of their family to discuss how the celebration of a particular time has evolved in their own household.
- Collect stories from other cultures that can be represented chronologically and consider creating personal introductions to them which relate to individual/family experiences (e.g. the story of The Gunpowder Plot links to a personal account of what happens on Bonfire Night). Like Jaffrey, narrate this in the present continuous (rather than the past) tense: 'Scores of workmen descend on the house'; 'We run outside and begin lighting the lamps'.
- Look at the entries in the appendix, explaining the pronunciation and origin of names related to Indian culture. Provide similar entries for other cultures (e.g. 'Guy Fawkes', 'Mohammed', 'Dauphin', etc.).

Links to other texts

Look at other collections of myths and legends, such as:
Celtic Myths by Sam McBratney (Macdonald).
The Book of Mythology by David Bellingham (Kingfisher).

EXPLORING CHARACTER

Make a collection of characters.

Choose six characters from *Seasons of Splendour*.

Put one in each of the character boxes below.

Write:

their names

the story they appear in

words that describe them in the text

what you think about them.

Character card 1
Name
Story
Words in the text
I think

Character card 2
Name
Story
Words in the text
I think

Character card 3
Name
Story
Words in the text
I think

Character card 4
Name
Story
Words in the text
I think

Character card 5
Name
Story
Words in the text
I think

Character card 6
Name
Story
Words in the text
I think

PICTURE TO TEXT

Find three colour pictures in *Seasons of Splendour* from stories you don't know.

Fill in the grid below, showing what you see and think when you look at these pictures.

Page	What I can see in the picture	What I think is happening

Mr William Shakespeare's Plays

*Written and illustrated by
Marcia Williams*

Walker Books ISBN 0-744-55502-7

Learning opportunities

Range: Shakespeare tales, classic texts.
Themes: Shakespeare's comedies and tragedies.
Terminology: archaic language; formal/ informal; proverbs; quotation; reported/direct speech.

Outline

The book contains cartoon strip versions of Shakespeare plays. Each tale includes a narrative. The pictures are accompanied by Shakespearean quotes and around the texts are comments from an imaginary audience showing individuals' responses to parts of the plays.

Ways of working

Text

Comparing language
Make comparisons between the comic-strip versions and the Standard English text. After reading one of the stories, select one scene that can be compared with an original Shakespeare text, for example, the witches' scene from *Macbeth*. Read through the comic page based on the cauldron again and discuss what is happening. Explore the idea of witches having special powers and creating charms. You then provide pupils with a copy of the original witches' scene (see photocopiable). Read this to them. Follow this with discussion of the rhyme and rhythm of the extract.

Ingredients
Instruct pupils in pairs to list some of the ingredients that have been placed in the cauldron. Point out from the picture book the reference to 'poison'd entrails' and give them two examples from the original (for example, 'Toe of frog', 'eye of newt'). Explain why Shakespeare chose these ingredients, noting that they are parts of once living creatures and ones that are generally viewed as repugnant. Ask them to write on the cauldron their own choice of gruesome ingredients using the original as a model.

Passage of time
Explore different possibilities for conveying the passage of time. There are many opportunities for developing children's understanding of how time is conveyed in these comic strips (for example, the play within *Hamlet* that tells of an event which took place prior to the opening of *Hamlet*). One explicit technique is used in *The Tempest*. Read *The Tempest* to your pupils and focus upon the opening picture box. In this box it is made evident that the story that is to follow had taken place during the previous 12 years. Encourage pupils to look at the pictures to see how Miranda was a child of three in Prospero's account of how they had been cast away on the island. Point out the illustrator's use of one colour to show that these events took place in the past. Ask pupils to use this flashback model for their own writing. Working in pairs, ask them to each think of a predicament in which a character could be found (e.g. shipwrecked, trapped in a cage, lost in tunnels) and then to explain to their partner how they came to be in that situation. This could act as a stimulus to story-writing.

Flow diagram
Read *Hamlet* with your class, indicating the different stages of plot development.

Comment on how the pictures relate to the written text, stopping to ask pupils what is happening in the pictures. Then explain the narrative as follows.

1. *Establishing the situation.* Hamlet's father is dead. A ghost tells Hamlet that his uncle Claudius was the murderer.
2. *Problem.* The ghost tells Hamlet to take revenge. Hamlet must decide if the ghost is telling the truth.
3. *Resolving the problem.* Hamlet organises a play for Claudius to watch. The play presents the murder of Hamlet's father as described by the ghost. Claudius' reaction to this play indicates his guilt.
4. *Climax and conclusion.* Hamlet waits for the opportunity to kill Claudius. Claudius is killed and so is Hamlet.

This model can be presented as a flow diagram, with one event leading to another along a succession of arrows. Ask pupils in small groups to complete a flow diagram for one of the other plays, using the headings shown in the *Hamlet* example. Next to each stage pupils can include appropriate Shakespearean quotes.

Sentence

To explore some of the differences between spoken and written English, encourage pupils to compare the audience's comments from one story with the Standard English narrative. Help pupils to identify some of the main differences, such as the use of contractions (where's, she's) and colloquialisms (he hasn't got the bottle). Pupils can select a section of a play and create appropriate audience's comments of their own. This should encourage close reading of the text. Collect a class list of audience comments and point out the typical features of informal spoken language.

Extension

- Rewrite one of the comic strips in a modern setting using the central ideas. The children need to decide where to set their version, finding a modern setting that offers the isolation of an island for a version of *The Tempest* or thinking where a modern-day Hamlet would reside.

Word notes

Ask pupils to make a list of some of the archaic words used in the quotations from the play (e.g. ay, thou). Show them how footnotes work in most published Shakespeare texts and ask them to write some footnotes for some of the terms they have gathered, drawing on the context of the word for their understanding of what it means.

- Write a message in a bottle from Miranda recounting her experiences on the island. At what stage could it be written and what would she say about her experiences on the island?
- Investigate quotes from the illustrations, seeking them out in original texts of the plays. Ask children to read some of the lines around these quotes, drawing on the understanding they will have gained from reading the picture book version.
- Sort the plays into groups. Ask children to devise a set of criteria for sorting the plays into two groups. It could be 'happy' and 'sad' or 'magical' and 'non-magical'. Ask children to do this in groups of four and then compare the various criteria used to see if particular ones stand out as widely used.
- Get children to give a similar treatment to another text, retelling it in prose passages complemented by illustrations in which they have fun with the speech bubbles. They could even include an audience around the edges.

Links to other texts

Look at other retellings of the plays, such as Leon Garfield's *Shakespeare Stories*.

MACBETH PIECE

Act IV

Scene 1

A dark cavern. In the middle a fiery cauldron. Thunder. Enter the three **Witches**.

1st Witch Thrice the brinded cat hath mewed.

2nd Witch Thrice, and once the hedge-pig whined.

3rd Witch Harpier cries: 'Tis time, 'tis time.

1st Witch Round about the cauldron go:
In the poisened entrails throw.
Toad, that under cold stone
Days and nights has thirty-one
Sweltered venom sleeping got,
Boil thou first i'th' charmed pot!

All Double, double toil and trouble;
Fire, burn; and cauldron, bubble.

2nd Witch Fillet of a fenny snake,
In the cauldron boil and bake:
Eye of newt and toe of frog,
Wool of bat and tongue of dog,
Adder's fork and blind-worm's sting,
Lizard's leg and howlet's wing
For a charm of powerful trouble,
Like a hell-broth boil and bubble.

All Double, double toil and trouble:
Fire, burn; and cauldron, bubble.

3rd Witch Scale of dragon, tooth of wolf,
Witch's mummy, maw and gulf
Of the ravined salt-sea shark,
Root of hemlock digged i'th' dark,
Liver of blaspheming Jew,
Gall of goat and slips of yew
Slivered in the moon's eclipse,
Nose of Turk and Tartar's lips
Finger of birth-strangled babe
Ditch-delivered by a drab,
Make the gruel thick and slab:
Add thereto a tiger's chaudron,
For th'ingredience of our cauldron

All Double, double toil and trouble;
Fire, burn; and cauldron, bubble.

2nd Witch Cool it with a baboon's blood,
Then the charm is firm and good.

- Read this scene with two other children

- Underline any animals in green

- Shade over rhyming words in blue

- Circle your ten favourite potion ingredients

CHARACTER CROSS-SECTION

Look through the plays

In each of them find your favourite character and explain what you like about them.

Play	Favourite character is _____ because
Play	Favourite character is _____ because
Play	Favourite character is _____ because
Play	Favourite character is _____ because
Play	Favourite character is _____ because
Play	Favourite character is _____ because
Play	Favourite character is _____ because

4 Entering imaginary worlds

Listen: In the days of yesteryear, life still blossomed now and again into a kind of dreamworld. Storytellers thus were free to lavish upon their creations liberties that had nothing to do with lies.

(Chamoiseau 1994, p.5)

In this chapter we look at picture books that can transport us into imaginary worlds. They have helped us to communicate to children the potential of stories as a vehicle for fantasy and for investigating possible worlds. Some of the texts, like *The Blue Balloon*, begin in everyday settings, while others are located in history, myth or popular fantasy. In our selection here we have tried to incorporate the following themes:

- the daydream – from everyday reality to imagined worlds, and back;
- the parallel world of magic and mystery;
- swashbuckling adventure;
- historical fiction;
- myths and legends.

The titles in this chapter

Mick Inkpen	*The Blue Balloon*
Jonathan London	*Let the Lynx Come In*
Michael Rosen and Helen Oxenbury	*We're Going on a Bear Hunt*
Colin McNaughton	*Captain Abdul's Pirate School*
Alfred Noyes and Charles Keeping	*The Highwayman*
Marcia Williams	*Greek Myths for Young Children*

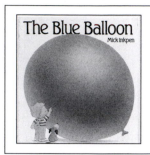

The Blue Balloon

Written and illustrated by Mick Inkpen.

Hodder Children's Books ISBN 0-340-55884-9

Learning opportunities

Range: stories about fantasy worlds.

Themes: magical transformations.

Terminology: narrator; setting; sentence; adjective.

Outline

The book involves a blue balloon that does magical things, e.g. it becomes square, is indestructible, takes the narrator to the moon and eventually turns into a rainbow-coloured balloon. The book features expanding, pull-out pages as the balloon grows.

Ways of working

Text

Narrator's voice
The book is written in the first person. Discuss this with children, e.g. ask them who is telling the story. How do they know? Move on to develop the narrator's character. Ask the children if they can give him a name. Move on to thinking about where he lives, who he lives with and so on. Once the children have built up a strong profile of the boy, ask them, in a shared writing session, to write a sequel to *The Blue Balloon* involving the boy and the dog. Their story can also be told in the first person. Share other books with the children that are told in the first person and compare them with third-person texts.

Comparing common themes in stories
Explore the conventions of fantasy stories, as shown in this book. *The Blue Balloon* is based in the everyday world and takes the characters on fantastic adventures but makes sure that they get back home safely. Ask the children to pick out and list the things about the story that are fantastic. Ask the children if they can think of other books that do this, e.g. *Where the Wild Things Are*; *Whatever Next?* Ask them to make a list of the similarities and differences between these texts (e.g. 'the characters go on journeys' would be a similarity, 'they go to different places' would be a difference). Children can then write their own fantasy story, drawing on some of the similarities they have seen within the genre.

Balloon label
In a shared/guided writing session, ask the children to choose a significant incident from the story, e.g. the balloon turning multi-coloured. Ask them to write a packaging label for a balloon like this. This would be the label that goes on the packet, including instructions for use, place of origin and warnings about safety (e.g. 'May fly away! Let go after 1.5 metres. Do not use under low flying aircraft').

Page formats

Look at how the various changes to the balloon lead to new page formats, e.g. extending pages. Children can try making their own magical transformation to a picture, in the style of *The Blue Balloon*.

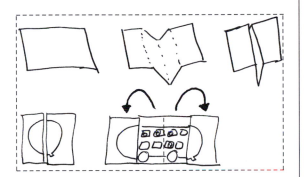

Sentence

Develop the children's understanding of adjectives. Ask them to make a list of all the words which describe the balloon throughout the book. Can they think of alternative words to the ones used in the text? Ask the children to play an 'add an adjective' game. Look at one of the magical balloons in the book. How many adjectives can they think of to describe the balloon in that picture? Each child adds one in turn, e.g. the blue balloon; the big, blue balloon; the big, square, blue balloon.

As they work towards creating their own balloon story, this activity can stimulate children to produce their own balloons. They can make a list of describing words, drawing on a wide range of adjectives that are not necessarily linked to balloons (e.g. woolly, scary). These can then be drawn upon as they think of the way in which their balloon could change in their story.

Extension

- Give each child a balloon. Ask the children to write a description of their balloon using the structure, e.g. 'My balloon is . . .', 'My balloon feels

Word notes

Ask the children to make a glossary of new words they meet in the book and write definitions for them, e.g. 'indestructible'.

Focus on the phoneme 'oo' as in 'balloon'. Cut out balloon shapes and ask the children to write words with the 'oo' sound in these shapes. They can display these by hanging them from the ceiling. Ask the children to make a sentence using as many of the 'oo' words as they can, e.g. 'The balloon soon flies to the moon'.

like . . .', 'My balloon can . . .', 'My balloon goes . . .', etc. Paste the poem onto the balloon and hang them up!

- Write the sequel to the story. This time, the main character has a Yo-Yo. What does this Yo-Yo do? Again, children can do the two things of listing where the Yo-Yo could go and using adjectives to describe the way in which it could change.

- Make a zigzag strip. Each section describes an action which the boy does to the balloon, based on the relevant section of the text (i.e. I squeezed it/squashed it). Write the relevant verb on each section of the strip. Draw a figure doing each of the actions to accompany the written text.

- Write a letter to balloon manufacturers, requesting the most wonderful types of balloons you can imagine. For instance, instead of being multi-coloured, could balloons be striped/spotted, etc?

Links to other texts

Fantasy/adventure stories which are rooted in the 'real' world: *Where the Wild Things Are*; *Whatever Next*; *Under Sammy's Bed*.

KIPPER'S DIARY

Fill in some notes about a trip to the moon.

The day I went to the moon

How I got there

What the moon looked like

What else I saw on the moon

What we did on the moon

How I felt when I got home

DIFFERENT BALLOONS

Write a description of a balloon. It could be 'a big red balloon'. Draw your balloon in the space underneath.

Try using more than one describing word for each balloon.

Words to describe your balloon

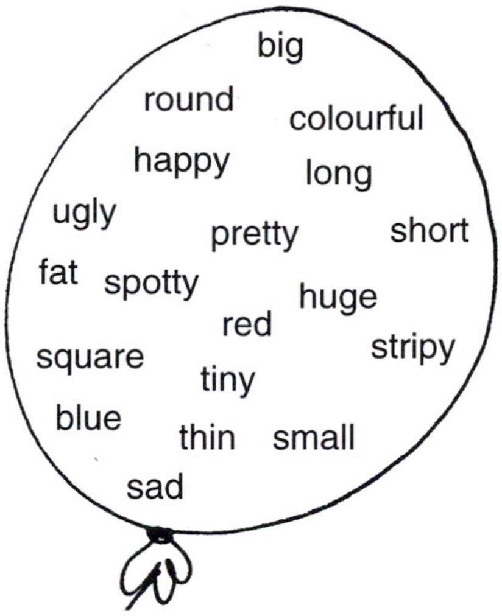

big
round colourful
happy long
ugly
pretty short
fat spotty
huge
red
square stripy
tiny
blue
thin small
sad

a _____

balloon

a _____

balloon

a _____

balloon

a _____

balloon

a _____

balloon

a _____

balloon

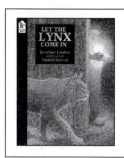

Let the Lynx Come In

Written by Jonathan London and illustrated by Patrick Benson.

Walker Books ISBN 0-744-56041-1

Learning opportunities

Range: adventure stories; descriptive poetry.

Themes: adventurous journeys; child as explorer of 'new worlds'; adult/child relationships.

Terminology: adventure stories; poems based on observation and the senses; story setting.

Outline

This is a small boy's account of a stay in the Alaskan wilderness with his father – a place he has never been to before. His inability to sleep leads him to wonder about the possible wild animals lurking outside the log cabin. One such animal, a lynx, arrives at the cabin door and takes him on a fantasy journey.

Ways of working

Text

Looking at story elements
Read the story to the children, highlighting the 'three-part' structure of the text: before the journey–the journey–after the journey. Collect words and phrases which highlight these three features and write them on appropriate three-colour backgrounds (orange, blue and orange) reflecting those in the story. Ask the children to suggest further appropriate words and phrases that are not in the story to reflect the three stages. Plot a similar journey in another environment, suggesting how a story could move through three locations and gathering the words that could be associated with each (e.g. jungle, desert, moon, etc.).

Writing a descriptive poem
Get the children to list contrasting words that are associated with the text. These could be actual words from the text, such as 'fire' and 'ice', or oppositions of their own devising, such as 'awake' and 'asleep'.

Look at some photographs or pictures of contrasting landscapes around the world. Make some antonyms (words for opposites) to label the opposite features of these settings.

Exploring characterisation
Use the illustrations and the words in the story to create three lists which tell you about the characters: the boy; his father; the lynx. Initially, select words that are actually in the text (e.g. can't sleep (boy); snores (his father); quiet (the lynx). Then get the children to suggest words and phrases that are not in the text (e.g. frightened (boy); content and cosy (his father); mysterious (the lynx)).

Awake and asleep
Did the boy dream the encounter with the lynx? Through a combination of exploration in the text and their own ideas about the story children can debate

this. They could compare the story with others, such as *Krindlekrax* by Philip Ridley or Maurice Sendak's *Where the Wild Things Are*, in which the boundaries between being awake and asleep are blurred.

Sentence

Focus on the use of the first person ('I...') throughout the story. Looking at sections of the story ask children to say them in the third person ('He hears a scratching...'). Look at the use of the present tense and ask children to try saying sections of the text in the past tense ('I heard a scratching...').

Bringing together the use of the first person and the present tense, construct a narrative with the children that makes use of these elements. Use an evocative theme for the story, such as entering a spooky house, and try devising a few sentences that would appear in such a narrative (e.g. 'I push the creaking door').

Extension

- Look at the dedication in the front of this book. It could prompt an investigation into the work of Alaskan poet, John Haines. Look at the dedications in other texts and see what sort of things writers say at this point in their stories.
- Look at encylopaedia entries on the lynx (and possibly compare with other animals). Look at similar entries about other animals and, bearing in mind what these other animals are like and where they live, plot similar encounters with different animals in different settings.

Word notes

Look at the use of alliteration (consonant sounds repeated for effect) and assonance (vowel sounds repeated for effect) in the story. For example, 'bare black branch' is an example of alliteration, whereas 'open it a crack, then jump back...A WILDCAT' is an example of a repeated 'a' sound, a use of assonance. Ask the children to try finding examples of sounds repeated in close proximity to each other that affect the reading of the text.

- Consider extracts from stories that have approached similar 'main character in an unfamiliar setting' situations, e.g. *Where the Wild Things Are* (Maurice Sendak). How do characters react to the different circumstances in which these stories place them?
- Brainstorm lists of verbs that describe the actions of particular creatures, e.g. cats: climb, miaow, purr, sleep; dogs: bark, chase, growl.

Links to other texts

This story fits well with stories that build bridges between familiar worlds and fantasy. Kit Wright's *Tigerella* and the follow-up *Dolphinella* have a similar shape and also involve magical animals. Raymond Briggs's *The Snowman* and Maurice Sendak's *Where the Wild Things Are* follow a similar structure. With older children you could use this text in conjunction with extracts from the Narnia books, Bel Mooney's *The Stove Haunting*.

LET THE LYNX COME IN

Imagine that a fantastic creature or character walked into your life!

Where could they take you?

What would you do?

e.g. With *a centaur* I would go to *ancient Greece* and we would *fly over Mount Olympus and wave at Zeus.*

With _____ I would go to _____

and we would _____

_____

With _____ I would go to _____

and we would _____

_____

With _____ I would go to _____

and we would _____

_____

With _____ I would go to _____

and we would _____

_____

OPPOSITE SIDES

Think what it is like inside and outside the cabin.

What would you see and hear?

How would it feel?

What happens inside and outside?

We're Going on a Bear Hunt

Written by Michael Rosen and illustrated by Helen Oxenbury.

Walker Books ISBN 0-744-51135-6

Learning opportunities

Range:　　poems with patterned and predictable structures; settings in stories.

Themes:　journeys; places.

Terminology:　setting; adjective.

Outline

As a family undertake a Bear Hunt they travel through varied terrain. On finding the bear they have to head quickly for home.

Ways of working

Text

Sequencing the settings
Prepare a set of cards with names of the settings in the story, e.g. river, snowstorm. Read through the story and, as each setting is encountered, ask one of the children to stand up and hold the card with that label. As the story progresses a line of children forms, showing the settings. At the end of the story the family race past each of these, so the line is gone through once again but in reverse order. Having read the story in this way ask the children in the line to sit down. Give the cards to a new row of children, giving any card to any child (i.e. out of order with the plot of the story). Ask the rest of the class to give instructions to this new line until they think they have got the original order (e.g. 'Carl needs to come

first', 'Chloe changes places with Sobia'). Check this new order with the book. If it isn't right, try a new line of children.

Learn the rhyme
Whether you plan for them to learn it or not, children inevitably will. There are traditional actions for this (such as treading in a plodding way for the mud) but it's far better to devise your own ideas. Children can learn the rhyme and then try saying it with the rhythm of the words. This can provide an excellent stimulus for a movement lesson.

Map the story
Ask the children to draw a map of the story. Begin by making a list of the settings on the board. Ask them if they can remember how each setting was described. From this list children create their own maps of the story, placing the locations on. They can also write on the adjectives used to describe the various features.

Other settings, adjectives and noises
Devise other settings where a Bear Hunt could take place. These can be close to home (an urban Bear Hunt can be an interesting thing) or in more exotic locations, such as deserts and rainforests. If children undertake this activity working in groups of eight they can end up with their own sequenced Bear Hunt. For each location they need to think of a name and descriptive word. For example, the 'road' could be 'a busy, smelly road'. They also have to think of the noises used to describe

the characters' journey through the location, so the road could be undertaken with noises like 'beep . . . vroom, beep . . . vroom, beep . . . vroom'.

Other things in the cave

The discovery of the bear takes place as the children work out they are encountering the eyes and the nose, etc. Children can devise their own cave encounter with their own frightening creature. Lions, aliens, monsters, dragons – any of these could make an interesting encounter in a dark cave! Children need to devise how they would gradually realise what they are encountering in their cave. Here, again, they don't just name the thing they feel, hear or smell; they also need to provide that adjective, as the book does with the parts of the Bear. A dragon could be encountered as 'lots of crinkly scales, a smelly hot breath, long, pointed tail . . . it's a dragon!' These could be written in cave-shaped pieces of paper as part of a display.

Sentence

The book is rich in its use of adjectives. For each setting there is a rhythmical pair of adjectives; for example the snowstorm is 'a swirling whirling snowstorm'. These can be looked at before the poem is read, listing the settings on a sheet of paper and asking children to think of words that would describe them. One aspect of children's use of adjectives that comes out in this is the way that, as they develop their use of this word class, they often do so with ones relating to their own senses and sensations. So whereas the book uses the description above, children will often describe it as 'scary' or 'cold'. You can use the opportunity provided by this list of locations to extend children's use of adjectives, prompting them to try and describe what the actual setting, would look like. Once you have a few potential descriptions of

Word notes

Look at the sounds used in the words that describe progress through the different obstacles, such as 'squelch' and 'splosh'. Selecting one of these words, pick out some of its sounds and ask children to think of other words with that sound. So for a word like 'splosh' children could try listing other words with the 'sp' or 'sh' sounds. When it comes to devising their own locations, children can devise elaborate sounds of their own and consider how they could use their understanding of letter sounds to represent these new words.

each setting, embark on reading and compare the text's adjectives with your own.

Extension

- Using various instruments, children can devise a musical score for the rhyme. They need to pick instruments that suit the various locations. Alternatively, they could use the locations they have devised and orchestrate a path through these.
- Children could write a note from the Bear to the family. This could be an angry request not to pester him again. Alternatively, it could be that the Bear wants to explain why she gave chase! They could extend this to writing a reply to the Bear from one of the children.
- Drawing on their own ideas for Bear Hunt locations, children could create actions and dramatise their ideas. They could then try teaching their new action Bear Hunt to other children.

Links to other texts

Other books using traditional rhymes include *Each Peach Pear Plum* by Janet and Allan Ahlberg, and *Little Rabbit Foo Foo* by Michael Rosen.

BEAR HUNT WORDS

Each of the *Bear Hunt* places has words to describe it and a special noise. Can you find the adjectives (describing words) and noises for each place?

Try to do this without looking in the book

Uh-uh! Grass!

_____ _____ grass

Noise:

Uh-uh! A river!

A _____ _____ river

Noise:

Uh-uh! Mud!

_____ _____ mud

Noise:

Uh-uh! A forest!

A _____ _____ forest

Noise:

Uh-uh! A snowstorm!

A _____ _____ snowstorm

Noise:

Check your version with the book.

BEAR HUNT MAKER

Think of your own place along a Bear Hunt route.

It could be outdoors (e.g. a swamp, a desert) or indoors (e.g. a spooky house, a library).

Use the frames below to make your own Bear Hunt pages. Put a noise in the noise box.

Uh-uh! _____!

_____!

We can't go over it.

We can't go under it.

Oh no!
We've got to go through it!

—— Noise box ——

Uh-uh! _____!

_____!

We can't go over it.

We can't go under it.

Oh no!
We've got to go through it!

—— Noise box ——

Captain Abdul's Pirate School

Written and illustrated by Colin McNaughton.

Walker Books ISBN 0-744-54702-4

Learning opportunities

Range: adventure stories; stories by the same author.
Themes: rules and regulations; gender roles; characterisation.
Terminology: fantasy adventure; vocabulary; exclamation marks.

Outline

A diary account of a young child's experiences as a newcomer at the Pirate School. The teachers are a motley crew of buccaneers who encourage robbing, cheating and making fake money. One night the pirates plan to kidnap the children and demand ransom money from their parents. Fortunately, they are overheard and the children stage a mutiny. The story ends in the West Indies, where the children do just as they please – Maisy Pickles is revealed as the author of the diary.

Ways of working

Text

Talking about the visual impact of the book
This story is set in the fantasy world of pirates and this is partly conveyed to the reader through the visual elements of the book. Ask children to identify the type of story before reading. They can list the ways in which this information is conveyed and the effect it has. For example, the front cover shows Captain Abdul with all the characteristics of the story book pirate (hook, eye-patch, earring, wooden leg, etc.), the end papers are like a pirate scarf and the back cover shows a skull and cross bones. The illustrations also use comic book conventions and speech bubbles.

Looking at the work of Colin McNaughton
After reading the story, compare this with other books by Colin McNaughton (e.g. *Have You Seen Who's Just Moved in Next Door to Us?*, see page 28). Discuss the techniques that Colin McNaughton uses to create a sense of surprise and movement in the sequence where Alright Jack fires the canon. Compare this with illustrations from *Boo!* or *Suddenly!* (also by Colin McNaughton). Ask children to contrast this style with the work of Anthony Browne (e.g. *Zoo*).

Fantasy worlds
By looking at the way Captain Abdul is represented, children can explore the characteristics of the pirate stereotype. Creating a 'Wanted' poster will encourage close study of the words and images used to depict the pirate Captain. The ways in which children in the story inadvertently discover the school rules can help us to see that the action takes place in a fantasy world in which normal conventions are reversed. Children can be asked to draw up the school rules for the Pirate School – and also what punishments could await those who break them. The fantasy characters in the story are seen through the eyes of Maisy Pickles, who records the events in her diary, and this can lead us into talking about narration. The diary creates a familiar structure through which we view unusual events. This concept could be extended by asking children to record

the same events from Captain Abdul's point of view in the school log book.

Sentence

Collect examples of how speech is represented in the story (e.g. 'We'll get yer kit stowed away ooh-arrgh'; 'I'm Yardarm Pitts that's me name'). Use these to look at how pronunciation is suggested through spelling and abbreviation. Children could compile a phrase book to help new pupils in the Pirate School.

You can also look at the way phrases in parentheses are used to provide additional information and how this is used to humorous effect (as an 'aside').

Word notes

The choice of vocabulary adds to the fantasy setting. Experiment with the verb forms in 'stow away', 'walk the plank', 'pay ransom', 'stage a mutiny'. How might 'put away' or 'have a mutiny' sound?

Look at specific 'pirate' vocabulary and make up dictionary definitions (e.g. buccaneers, hammocks, cannon, etc.).

List the different verbs used for 'tricked' (e.g. double-crossed, duped, etc.).

Collect pirate exclamations (e.g. Ooaargh! Avast!, etc.).

Extension

- Think about rules and why we have them – talking about the current school rules and sanctions that apply. You can link this in with changes in school rules. Looking at the school log book can often be quite informative!
- Use the photocopiable to look at The Pirate School Rules. Extend this by creating a Pirate School Brochure and a letter to parents to introduce the school.
- The story ends in a sort of tropical paradise in which children do as they please. Children can be asked to write and talk about their own 'ideal world'.
- Conduct class research into historical facts about pirates and think about how and why their exploits have become popular fantasy material. Relate this to children's experience of 'swashbuckling' films like *Hook*.
- *Captain Abdul's Pirate School* is written in diary form. Ask children to compile Captain Abdul's diary.

Links to other texts

Captain Abdul appears in a number of other Colin McNaughton books. There is the companion volume *Jolly Roger* as well as 'guest' appearances in other titles (e.g. *Have You Seen Who's Just Moved in Next Door to Us?*). Look for how pirates are represented in other texts, from *Peter Pan* and *Treasure Island* to *Captain Pugwash* and the work of Margaret Mahy (*The Great Piratical Rumbustification* and *The Man Whose Mother Was a Pirate*). There are also a lot of similarities between the books of Colin McNaughton and the work of the Ahlbergs. In fact McNaughton collaborated with Allan Ahlberg on the Red Nose Readers (e.g. *Help!*) and the sense of comic-book fun, fast action and word-play is clearly a shared interest. Close comparisons can be drawn between the brigands in the Ahlbergs' *It Was a Dark and Stormy Night* and Captain Abdul's pirates. Children could compare how Janet Ahlberg illustrates the brigands firing of a cannonball with Alright Jack's lesson on angles at the Pirate School.

SCHOOLS HAVE RULES

- All schools have rules.

- Sometimes they are written down.

- Use the book to make a list of the Pirate School's rules.

- Add some of your own.

Captain School Abdul's Rules.

1.
2.
3.
4.
5.
6.
7.
8.
9.
10.
11.
12.
13.

Punishments

1.

2.

3.

4.

PIRATE CLASSROOMS

Map out the classrooms in Captain Abdul's school.

Decide where to put different classes, living quarters and other cabins.

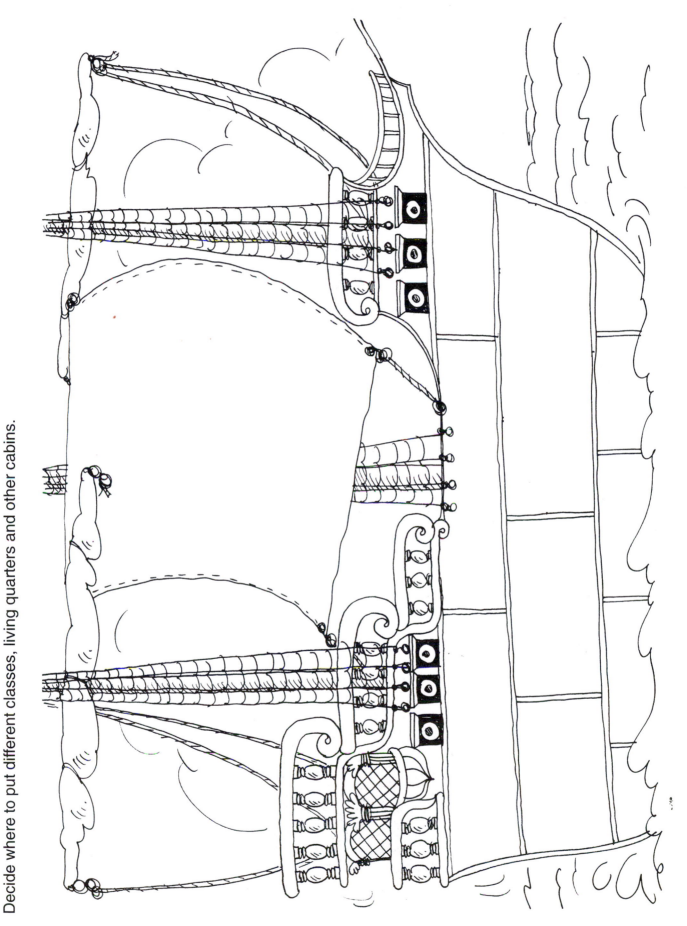

The Highwayman

Written by Alfred Noyes and illustrated by Charles Keeping.

Oxford University Press ISBN 0-192-72133

Learning opportunities

Range: narrative poem; historical text; classic text.
Themes: betrayal; loyalty; love; legends.
Terminology: narrator; viewpoint; rhyme; simile; metaphor; alliteration; assonance.

Outline

This dramatic poem is based upon the romantic relationship between a highwayman and a woman called Bess. The Highwayman informs Bess that he will return to her in the moonlight to avoid the authorities. Tim, a stable-hand, overhears the conversation and it is inferred that he informs the King's Red Coats because he is in love with Bess, leading to tragic consequences from which the legend of the Highwayman arises.

Ways of working

Text

Reading and rereading
This is a complex poem and merits a couple of readings to get the gist of the story. Read the poem *The Highwayman* to the class then involve the class in reading the poem a second time with pairs of pupils each reading a few lines, trying to capture the rhythm of the poem. Ask each pair to try and figure out what is happening in their section of the poem then, once the poem is completed, go through the pairings one at a time piecing together what happened.

Radio play
Explain that they are going to create a radio play based upon the poem. The children listen to a short radio play or recorded play of a story and identify the key features of this genre, such as sound effects and the way we rely on characters to tell us things we would see on a television version of the same piece. In their groups children can try composing a radio play version of *The Highwayman*, with appropriate sound effects. They may even have suggestions for music to accompany their drama. When the play has been written and rehearsed several times it is then to be taped and played back to the whole class. Discussion that ensued would focus upon the differences between the poem and the radio play.

Poetic language
Explain to children the meaning of the terms:

- alliteration: the repetition of consonant sounds for effect in a poem (e.g. the repetition of the 's' sound in 'she stood up, straight and still');
- assonance: the repetition of vowel sounds for effect in a poem (e.g. repetition of the long 'i' sound in 'eyes grew wide');
- similes: where something is directly likened to another using the words 'as' or 'like' (e.g. 'face burnt like a brand', 'shot him down . . . like a dog on the highway');
- metaphors: where something is described in terms of another thing (e.g. when 'blanket of snow' describes the snow in terms normally used for bed linen). Other examples include the description of 'when the road was a gypsey's ribbon'.

Split children into groups and, on reading the picture book, ask different groups to look out for one of these aspects and find two examples of their particular use of poetic language.

Imparting the news
Children can create written accounts of these events, produced by other characters. One particular character of interest is whoever told the Highwayman the news about Bess. How did this person hear the news and how did he or she feel about passing it on? What was the reaction of the Highwayman?

Moonlight
Explore the theme of moonlight in the poem. Ask children to make notes of the different places where it occurs and who refers to it and then ask them to write out some short notes on how the word is used in the poem.

Exploring the passage of time
Provide children with a list of the main events (e.g. Highwayman riding, Highwayman meets Bess, Tim overhears the conversation, Bess dies). These are then arranged in chronological order by the pupils in small groups, creating a time line for the poem. Questions can be raised about the last section of the poem. Where would this be placed, as it is an event that keeps occurring?

Sentence

Focus on the verbs in the poem. Organise the pupils into groups of four and allocate each one the following characters: the Highwayman, Bess, soldiers. Each group is then to identify a selection of verbs that are particularly linked to their character (e.g. the Highwayman – riding, clattered, whistled; Bess – twisted, writhed, stretched). Ask pupils what these suggest about the characters (e.g. the freedom of the Highwayman). Develop this exercise by giving key verbs to the

Word notes

Explore the use of archaic words with your class. As you read the poem you could identify archaic terms like 'casement' and 'thee'. Ask the pupils what this contributes to the text. Pupils are asked to keep a glossary of archaic words. You then request that they write a diary entry as if they are Tim. This will include at least four archaic words from the glossary and thus help to give a sense of the period in which it is set.

pupils and ask them to list alternatives (e.g. the man walked/ hobbled/sprinted down the road). Then ask the class what each verb suggests about the subject.

Extension

- Write a day in the life of a highwayman. What happens when he is not around during the day? Children can gather clues from the text ('if they press me sharply').
- Produce a newspaper article based upon the main events of the story. This can include quotes from some of the characters, such as the soldiers and Tim. Bear in mind that characters may not tell the truth to the press. Write up the story and devise an appropriate headline.
- The concept of heroes and villains can be explored. Who are the heroes and villains in this text? Although a criminal, children tend to side with the Highwayman. Can they explain why? Can they think of other 'anti-heroes'?

Links to other texts

Children can look at other night-time poems, such as 'The listeners' and 'The tide rises, the tide falls'. Both can be found in *Every Poem Tells a Story*, edited by Raymond Wilson (Puffin), along with many other examples of narrative poetry.

NARRATIVE IN POEM

Work with a partner.

In the boxes below write 6 events from *The Highwayman*.

Pick the main events.

Cut out your rectangles. Swap your rectangles with another pair of children's. Shuffle the piles and try putting the eight events back in order.

HIGHWAY CHARACTERS

Read through the poem and find two lines that describe these characters. Think of your own rhyming line to describe each character.

	Two lines from text
	My two lines

	Two lines from text
	My two lines

	Two lines from text
	My two lines

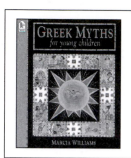

Greek Myths for Young Children

Written and illustrated by Marcia Williams.

Walker Books ISBN 0-744-53075-X

Learning opportunities

Range: traditional stories, myths, legends from a range of cultures.

Themes: mythology.

Terminology: word derivation; prefix; commentary; obituary; viewpoint.

Outline

This is a series of eight Greek myths told in cartoon-strip form. A humorous parallel to the main text is provided by the cartoon characters and their speech bubbles. The myths include the following: Pandora's Box; Arion and the Dolphins; Orpheus and Eurydice; The Twelve Tasks of Hercules; Daedalus and Icarus; Perseus and the Gorgon's Head; Theseus and the Minotaur; Arachne versus Athene.

Ways of working

Text

Writing in the voice and style of the text
Read the first story, 'Pandora's Box', highlighting the main features of the text (the illustrations, spoken language in speech and thought bubbles, and the narrative at the base of each illustration). Encourage the children to recognise the differences between the spoken text and the narrative (e.g. the use of exclamations, contracted forms of the verb, interjections, humour and a degree of formality in the speech bubbles). In columns written on the board, collect examples of the text alongside words from the voice bubbles. Ask the children to compare the level of formality.

Playing with speech bubbles
Look at how the speech bubbles are used in the illustrations to provide a humorous complement to the text. Select a part of one of the stories, and ask the children to devise some speech bubbles of their own showing what the characters could say at that point in the story. Children should be encouraged to include some of the features identified as characteristic of speech from the earlier activity, noting the way the speech bubbles allow the characters to issue humorous asides, etc.

Writing a journalistic report
Ask the children to adapt a text for a different readership and different purpose. This should be based on one of the stories (e.g. 'Orpheus and Eurydice'). Children will be expected to produce a newspaper article in an appropriate journalistic form. In preparation for this activity you should provide your class with models of newspaper articles and discuss key features such as headlines, illustrations, captions, layout, eye-witness accounts and points of view.

Children could work in pairs, staging imaginary interviews with characters from their chosen story, with one child taking on the role of the character and the other acting as interviewer.

Sentence

Contrast speech and writing, looking at the contrasts between the text under the pictures and the text in the speech bubbles. Ask children to devise their own pictures with the fuller sentences under the picture complemented by the speech in bubbles.

Extension

- Write one of the myths from the point of view of the villain or defeated monster, e.g. Theseus and the Minotaur from the Minotaur's point of view.
- Use first-person narrative. A character like the Minotaur might provide a completely different spin on the story – we could end up disliking Theseus!
- Take another, longer text and reproduce as a cartoon strip. For example, a classic novel could be presented in Marcia Williams's style,

Word notes

You can develop children's understanding of word derivations and the etymology of English words through activities on Greek prefixes and suffixes. Children can be asked to identify either the meaning of the root prefix from given words or produce examples of words from the given prefix and meaning (see photocopiable page).

complementing summaries of the action with wry speech bubbles.

- Write an alternative conclusion, either creating a 'happy' ending (e.g. Icarus survives), or one in which another character dies instead (e.g. the Minotaur kills Theseus).

Links to other texts

Look at other versions of the myths in different media. Look at other print versions such as: *The Puffin Classics Myths and Legends* and the *Orchard Book of Greek Myths*.

HERCULES' EPITAPH

Complete an epitaph showing the 12 tasks of Hercules . . .

Here lies Hercules who

1 _____
2. _____
3 _____
4 _____
5 _____
6 _____
7 _____
8 _____
9 _____
10 _____
11 _____
12 _____

Try filling the gravestones of other characters, e.g. Orpheus, Pandora.

Here lies
who

Here lies
who

GREEK ROOTS

Cut out these Greek roots. They are Greek words that have been used to make English words.

bio
(life)

geo
(earth)

tele
(far)

meter
(measure)

micro
(small)

phone
(sound)

Cut out these English words.
Match them up with their Greek roots.
Stick the words and roots together on a sheet of paper.

thermometer

biology

telescope

telephone

geography

microscope

Think of some other words using these roots.

5 Learning about ourselves and others

'Literature can be an effective way for children to learn about the diversity within and among cultures and to gain a sense of a country's ethnic history.

(Harada 1998, p. 19)

Picture books are a powerful way of showing difference and diversity. They can be particularly useful in providing positive images of children and their families in familiar and less familiar settings. They can provide images of those we can identify with as well as introducing us to alternative ways of life, beliefs and histories. Picture books in this chapter can of course be used in other ways, but we have found them useful to talk about the richness of our cultural lives and the different traditions in contemporary society.

Particular themes that can be explored include:

- the history and traditions of a particular social group;
- our families and relatives in other parts of the world;
- life in contemporary Britain;
- the lives of those in previous eras;
- religious beliefs and cultural traditions.

The titles in this chapter

Anne Marie Linden & Lynne Russell	*One Smiling Grandma*
Eileen Browne	*Handa's Surprise*
Sheldon Oberman & Ted Lewin	*Always Adam*
Scott Steedman	*The Egyptian News*

One Smiling Grandma

Written by Anne Marie Linden and illustrated by Lynne Russell.

Mammoth ISBN 0-780-749725006

Learning opportunities

Range: traditional, nursery and modern rhymes; rhymes; chants; action verses; predictable structures; patterned vocabulary.

Themes: numbers and counting; family life; grandparents; happiness.

Terminology: line; page; full stop; comma; sentence; rhyme.

Outline

A beautifully illustrated counting book set in the Caribbean. It uses simple rhyme following the pattern of 'One smiling grandma in a rocking chair, Two yellow bows tied on braided hair'. This is a modern counting rhyme with a predictable structure and patterned language in a Caribbean setting.

Ways of working

Text

Counting rhymes

Introduce your children to counting rhymes. Begin by reading or singing a familiar rhyme, such as 'One, two, three, four, five, once I caught a fish alive' or 'One, two buckle my shoe'. Then ask children to look for similarities as you read *One Smiling Grandma*. Discuss these similarities, making sure that the ideas of 'rhyme', 'number' and 'counting' are referred to. Reread the rhyme pausing to look at the pictures. Encourage children to point at and count the 'three humming birds', 'four steel drums', the 'five flying fish' and so on.

Exploring rhyme

Ask children if they know what a rhyme is – the idea that rhyming words sound the same may be sufficient explanation. Explain that you are going to list all the rhyming words from the text on the whiteboard. Give children a clue – the rhyming words are usually at the end of each line. Read the first page and ask which word is at the end of the line. Ask for a volunteer to point to that word. Write 'chair' on the board. In this way you will be able to list all the rhymes in the book. Encourage children to say each word and each rhyme as you write it. With luck someone will notice that 'air' and 'wares' don't quite rhyme. As follow-up, compose your own counting rhyme as a shared writing activity. The rhyme could be based on children's associations with grandparents. Start with the same first two lines, then ask for children's associations (e.g. 'three chocolate biscuits served on a plate'). Encourage children to think of rhymes for each number. Don't worry about the rhythm of your writing.

Grandparents

Talk about grandparents and what makes them happy. What would make the children's grandparents happy? Find out where children's grandparents were born and where they live now. Ask the children to work in small groups making their own 'smiling grandparent' list, compiled out of the various things that would make their own grandparents smile.

Sentence

Punctuation is used to help in the reading of this rhyme. Talk about the picture of three hummingbirds sipping sweet nectar. Encourage children to look at the illustration and to count the birds. Read the line on the page that acts as a caption.

Ask for a volunteer to point at the words as they are read. Draw the children's attention to the comma at the end of the line. See if anyone knows the term 'comma'. Read the next page together. Ask for a volunteer to point to the beginning and the end of the line. See if anyone knows where the full stop is. Repeat this with the following two pages, seeing if children can identify the comma and full stop. Explain that the comma suggests that there is a break in the sentence; the full stop signals the end and is usually given a longer pause in oral reading. To extend this work you could look at how punctuation is used in other familiar picture books. In choosing your examples try to make sure that you don't give the impression that lines always end with a full stop or comma. As follow-up work with a large version of the poem on a card or whiteboard, encourage children to read aloud and use a pointer to focus on the print. Ask the children to put their fingers on their lips each time you reach a comma or full stop. At first this will exaggerate the pauses but will illustrate your teaching point. Strips of 'post-its' can then be placed over commas and full stops and as you read the poems, children can predict the punctuation feature.

Extension

- Compare with other counting rhymes (e.g. 'This old man', 'The ants came marching one by one', 'Five currant buns'). Listen to counting rhymes in other languages. Compile a list of songs and rhymes that involve progression through counting. This could lead to the production of a tape or a performance of counting rhymes.
- Collecting, naming and tasting different fruit (at least eight kinds of fruit are shown in the market scene – also sugar apples and coconuts are described).

Word notes

Children can look for rhyming words that have a shared spelling pattern (e.g. chair/hair; beach/reach). These words can then be written on card and children can identify pairs. This could be developed into a form of the card game pelmanism.

Make matching games based on each number symbol, its written equivalent and the name and pictures of each of the objects (7 (seven) (conch shells)).

'Five flying fish' is an example of alliteration – focussing on the letter 'f' make up alliterative phrases. These alliterative phrases can be made into a class book.

Discuss the use of the prefix 'grand' as in 'grandpa', 'grandmother', 'granddaughter', etc. Talk about shortened forms (such as 'nan') and when and why we use them.

- Use as a starting point for children writing about family members ('I like my Grandma, She . . .'). Children could produce small books about a particular member of their family which may use rhyme.
- Talk about the emotions conveyed by smiling – discussion on what makes you feel happy. Make lists of the sorts of things that make them smile, or their parents . . . or teachers.

Links to other texts

This book works well with other rhymes, as some of the ideas above suggest. It also lends itself well to introducing other stories, rhymes and poems from the Caribbean (e.g. Valerie Bloom and David Axtell's *Fruits*). The fruit theme links well to Eileen Browne's picture book *Handa's Surprise*.

OTHER PLACES

- *One Smiling Grandma* is set in the Caribbean.
- The girl counts things that we may not often see.
- Draw six pictures and label them.

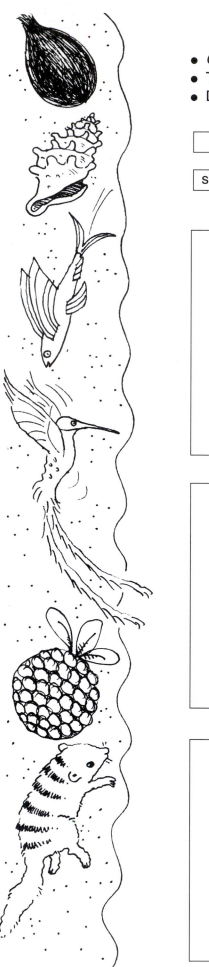

| coconuts | flying fish | a mongoose |

| sugar apples | hummingbirds | conch shells |

COUNTING

● Cut out and stick together in the right order.

One	Yellow bars
Five	smiling grandma
Two	hummingbirds
Four	flying fish
Three	steel drums

● Now draw five things for your own counting rhyme.

one _____
_____

two _____
_____

three _____
_____

four _____
_____

five _____
_____

Handa's Surprise

Written and illustrated by Eileen Browne.

Walker Books ISBN 0-744-55473-X

Learning opportunities

Range:	stories and rhymes; predictable and patterned language.
Themes:	friendship; food; surprises.
Terminology:	author; dedication; end pages; character; setting; sentence; full stop; question mark; speech marks.

Outline

Handa puts seven delicious fruits in a basket to take to her friend Akeyo as a surprise. But through a turn of events the surprise is Handa's.

Ways of working

Text

Cover features

Work with children on specific features of the cover. Draw their attention to author, title, blurb and end papers. You can use 'post-its' or card arrows to point these out. You can also point out the dedication and the author's acknowledgement of the people who helped her in her research for the story. You could use this to initiate discussion about the need to plan and research the stories we write. This page also explains that the children featured in the story are from the Luo tribe in Kenya. Discuss how some stories are rooted in people's daily lives and other stories feature fantasy worlds. Your children could be encouraged to identify stories they know that reflect their own daily lives.

The pictures tell a story

A key feature of this book is the way in which the written text contrasts with the illustrations. The written text gives Handa's point of view, as she wanders along and wonders which of the fruits Akeyo will like. The reader is invited to share the joke as each fruit is stolen by an animal. Ask children to tell this story to you from the pictures. You could also try reading the story to children before you show the pictures. Encourage children to compare this book with other stories which also use illustrations to add to the written text, e.g. *Come Away from the Water, Shirley, Rosie's Walk*.

Handa

Ask the children about the main character – what do we know or think about her? A technique called 'role on the wall' can be used here. Draw the outline of a body on a large piece of paper and ask the class to brainstorm about the character. Things that they think Handa feels, or attributes she has, can be written on the inside of the body outline (e.g. she is kind, she is surprised at the end of the story, she is a day-dreamer). On the outside of the body outline, you can write the words that children think of to describe what they know about the character's appearance and circumstances (e.g. Handa has braided hair, she wears flip-flops and she lives in a village in Africa). Children can then work on Handa in role-play to develop a deeper understanding of the character. For example, children can be 'hot-seated' as Handa. This involves one child taking on the role of Handa and other children asking them questions (e.g. why didn't you notice that all your fruit was being stolen? Why did you want to go and see Akeyo?).

Settings

The book lends itself to discussion of settings. Ask the children to guess where it is set, using questions which focus their attention on the depiction of heat, blue skies, the kinds of building materials used in the villages and so on. It should be stressed that you need to be aware of stereotypes here. For example, it is important to point out to children that Kenya also contains cities with houses and skyscrapers similar to ones they are familiar with.

Sentence

As the text is reread to the children, miss out the adjectives and encourage the children to think of words which describe the fruit. Use feely boxes and 'tasting trays' which feature the fruits used in the story to encourage both oral and written work. Encourage children to think of words to describe the textures and tastes they encounter. Using paper shaped like the fruits can enliven written work on adjectives!

Look at the use of question marks and encourage the children to write stories based around a similar pattern of questioning. Exclamation marks are used at the end of the book to express feelings of surprise. Similarly the word 'tangerines' appears in capital letters on the final page of the story to express surprise. Children could be encouraged to find other examples of this typographical feature in other books.

Word notes

As a vocabulary extension activity, children can list the names of fruit they have encountered for the first time in the story. Ask them to make other lists showing the spelling of other food types.

Extension

- Retell the story from the point of view of the animals as they see Handa pass by. Did they think about the fact that they were taking a fruit from her? Can they explain their actions? What did they think of their chosen fruit?
- Write a story about Handa's return journey – what adventures does she have along the way? Try to bring in some of the animals she met on the way. Would anything chase her? Could she get lost? Who might help her?
- Write the thank-you letter that Akeyo sends to Handa. If you send the children replies from Handa, the correspondence could go on for weeks!
- Carry out some research on the setting of the book (Kenya) and produce a 'fact-file' sheet or poster containing their findings.

Links to other texts

John Burningham's *The Shopping Basket* is very similar to *Handa's Surprise*. In *The Shopping Basket*, a boy has his shopping stolen by one animal after another as he walks home from the shops. The two books could be compared by the children and similarities and differences listed.

FRUITY WORDS

Cut out these words and stick them onto a sheet of paper.

Make the fruit description Handa uses in *Handa's Surprise*.

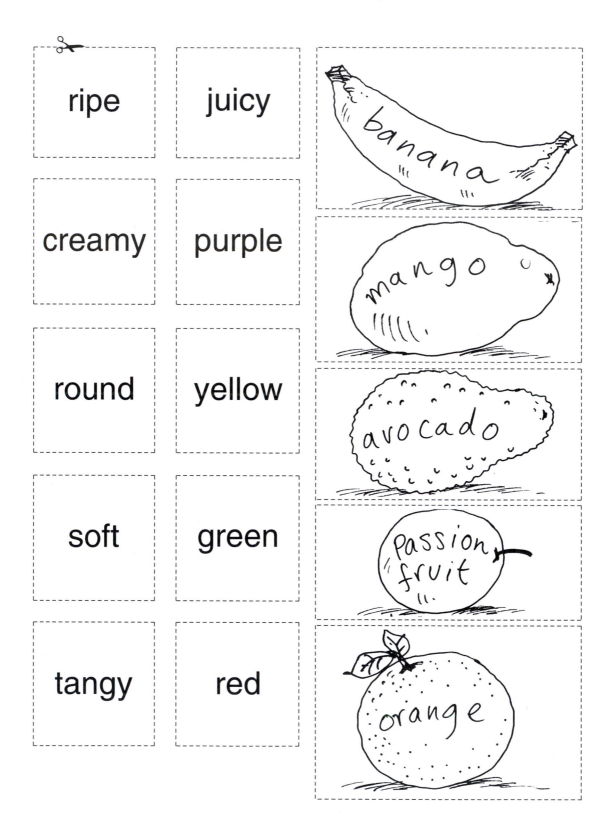

© Merchant & Thomas 1999, *Picture Books for the Literacy Hour.*

WHO STOLE WHAT

Read the story. Close the book. Try remembering what each animal stole. (You can look inside the front cover for a list of fruits.)

Write the fruit each animal stole alongside their picture.

What did the goat do?

_____

_____

_____

_____

_____

Always Adam

Written by Sheldon Oberman and illustrated by Ted Lewin.

Puffin ISBN 0-140-56331-8

Learning opportunities

Range: historical stories; stories from other cultures.

Themes: culture, tradition and religious belief across generations; identity; Jewish faith.

Terminology: historical narrative; dedication; symbolism; repetition; verb tense; temporal connectives.

Outline

This story charts the change and upheaval experienced by a Jewish family who emigrate from Russia to America in the middle of this century. The idea that 'some things change and some things don't' is used to explore the tension between adaptation and continuity, particularly in the context of religious tradition. The synagogue, the Hebrew language and the prayer shawl are motifs around which the story is woven. *Always Adam* is a simple historical narrative which presents us with sparse detail but plenty of emotion and food for thought.

Ways of working

Text

Looking at the passage of time
After a first reading of this book, look at the dedication. One of these is:'To my father's father, who I never knew'. Ask children to work out why this is included. Look at the use of black-and-white illustrations to illustrate people, places and events in the past. Point out how black-and-white photos of the family are displayed on the page where Adam is sewing new fringes on the prayer shawl. Ask children to identify how language is used to indicate the passage of time (e.g. many years ago, one day, then, finally, etc.). Children can make concertina books to illustrate the sequence of events in the story. Encourage them to use temporal connectives in their writing.

A sense of history
The contrast between 'old ways' and modern society is quite simply made on the first two pages. The contrasts recur later in the book. Children can represent this in chart form drawing information from both print and illustration. They can also be encouraged to add their own examples of how life might have changed for Adam's family. Using their own parents' and grandparents' ages and their knowledge of historical events, they should be able to suggest a time line for the story, mapping on real historical events.

Special places and special objects
The prayer shawl is used as a symbol of continuity in the story. Children can look for how the shawl reappears on the book cover, on the end papers and throughout

the book both through visual representation and through the written text. The book doesn't tell us a lot about the Jewish faith but children can look at the associations that are made with the prayer shawl, reading and writing in Hebrew and the synagogue, e.g. the synagogue is warm; they close their eyes; they sit close together; they talk about their family; they think about the past, etc.

Sentence

The passage of time is also reflected at sentence level. Children can look for noun phrases, verbs and connectives that show the passage of time (e.g. one day, then one day, every Saturday, then, finally). The repeated sentences 'The fringes changed. The collar changed. The cloth changed. Everything about it has changed' form a sort of chorus. Compare this with repetition in traditional and oral stories. Discuss the effect of repetition.

Extension

- Ask children to think about changes that have taken place since *their* grandparents' time. Invite a grandparent (or someone of that generation) into school. Children can interview them. This is particularly useful where the interviewee has similar experiences to those recounted in the story.
- The story leaves us wondering what might happen next. Children can write about what young Adam might do after the story (e.g. he might write to relatives in Russia, or visit; or he might

> **Word notes**
>
> Examine the nature of words that denote family relationships (e.g. father's father, grandfather's grandfather, son, grandson). This can be used to introduce the concept of prefixes and root words. You can build on this by representing these words on family trees. Also investigate words from other languages to describe family relationships.

forget about his family's traditions).
- Encourage the children to research the Jewish religion. They could write a letter arranging to visit the local synagogue or inviting the rabbi to school.
- Find out more about Hebrew language and script. Collect some texts that are written in Hebrew.
- Arrange to borrow items that are of significance to the Jewish tradition. A prayer shawl would be particularly useful to accompany the story.
- The story is entirely based around the male figures in the family. This is worth discussing. Children could write the story from a daughter's perspective.

Links to other texts

A number of other texts could be used. The work and themes of the author and illustrator can be seen through reading *The Day of Ahmed's Secret*. The theme of war and upheaval can be explored through Roberto Innocenti's *Rose Blanche*, *The Diary of Anne Frank* or *Zlata's Diary*.

FACT IN FICTION

'Adam was a Jewish boy in Russia.'

- *Always Adam* is fiction but is a story that is based on real events. It helps us to understand some of the things that are important to Jewish people.
- Use the book and illustrations to describe these words.

Hebrew is _____

_____

A synagogue is _____

_____

A prayer shawl is _____

_____

- Make a list of things from the book that are fact and those you think may be fiction.

Fact	Fiction

SOME THINGS CHANGE – AND SOME THINGS DON'T

● Make a list of things that change in Adam's life.

● Make a list of things that don't change in Adam's life.

● Now write a letter from Adam to his grandfather in Russia. Remember to ask about how things are in Russia and what changes have happened.

● Swap letters with a friend. Write a letter of reply from grandfather to Adam. Ask your friend to do the same.

The Egyptian News

Written by Scott Steedman.

Walker Books ISBN 0-744-54474-2

Learning opportunities

Range: non-fiction accounts of events; news reports; explanations; anecdotes; formal/informal language.

Themes: life in a different culture; events; attitudes.

Terminology: letters; persuasive texts; record of observations; poetic forms.

Outline

The Egyptian News is one of a series of texts which creates events from Egypt's history in newspaper format. The author argues that, if the Egyptians had actually produced a newspaper, it would have had much of the spirit of this one. Using a variety of different formats (reports, adverts, letters, instructions, surveys, etc.) it seeks to build up a portrait of life, as it was, in Egypt 3,000 years ago.

Ways of working

Text

Exploring authentic texts
Get the children to focus initially on actual newspapers. An ideal starting point is to look at the tabloid press. Collect examples of different ones: *The Mirror*, *The Sun*, *Daily Star*. Look at the way specific events are reported; compare different accounts of the same event. The focus needs to be on text organisation (paragraphing; order of events), sentence length (related to paragraph) and word selection (formal/informal). Some investigation of actual texts needs to happen, prior to looking at the way in which events are reported in *The Egyptian News*.

Looking at text types
The book gives several examples of different kinds of text: the majority are on reports of events, but there are also examples of adverts, surveys, instructions, and 'for sale' notices. The first focus needs to be on the nature of the 'report' structure. Compare and contrast how this operates in 'actual' tabloids (e.g. headlines, subheadings, paragraphing, etc.). Then relate to how the text is mostly organised in *The Egyptian News*. Look at the format of 'Introductory text' (e.g. Are you dying to know what goes on inside these mysterious embalming tents?) and 'Follow-up text' (e.g. 'Records from the mid-2500s BC suggest that . . .'). Translate this two-part structure into how this might have been written in terms of the tabloids.

Interviewing techniques
Several of the articles in the book (e.g. 'Mummy maker' and 'Tomb talk') take the form of written interviews. Use this format to create with the children other questions they might want to ask. They can then add the answers. They will need to research their answers using non-fiction texts on Ancient Egypt but, when it comes to producing the interview, they then have to tranform these facts into conversational style (e.g. 'And have you ever embalmed animals?'; 'Yes, of course. In my time I've done cobras, lizards, crocodiles – and even scarab beetles'). This could lead to a drama activity in which children present an Ancient Egyptian Chat Show.

Text types not included
The Egyptian News takes information that would often be covered in a history textbook and presents it in a different format, that of newspaper reportage.

Children can experiment for themselves with this idea by presenting information from this text in another format. For example, children can re-write the article 'Life on the river' as a cinquain poem. This is a poem like a haiku, with a set pattern of syllables in the lines. It involves placing the text in five lines, with two syllables in the first line, four in the second. The third line is made up of six syllables, the fourth of eight. The last line returns to two syllables. To produce an Egyptian Fact Cinquain, firstly select one person to focus on (e.g. farmer/scribe/ferryman).

Then identify a list of key words associated with that person and related to the time scale (e.g. October: work/mud/sow wheat; November: cut/ditch/channels/banks; March: harvest/repair damage). These phrases can then be reworked to produce an appropriate cinquain, for example:

Farmer
Cutting ditches
Sewing, watering earth
Harvesting, gathering the wheat
For food

Sentence

Look at several examples of adverts from the book. Focus initially on headlines: 'Weavers wanted', 'Fake-it furniture', etc. Look at the words that are selected to act as a heading for an advert. How crucial are they to the overall idea of the advert? Look in contemporary papers at adverts and the headings they use. Give children a selection of adverts with the heading or large title cut out of the text. Ask them to suggest a suitable title or slogan for the advert.

Extension

- This book is only one in a series (*The Aztec News*, *The Roman News*, etc). Their formats could be used to generate other aspects of history and geography (e.g. The Viking News). Ask the children to recall facts from a recent history project they have done and to use them to create their own newspaper format.

- Collect, and comment on, the text presented beneath each illustration in terms of form and purpose. Compare them with those you find in modern newspapers.

- Secure an exclusive interview with Rameses II for *The Egyptian News*. Make use of relevant information you might find in the current edition, then create questions and answers that tell you more about 'the man behind the mask'! This could form the basis of a subsequent interview with Rameses III. The two could then be compared (i.e. good/bad ruler).

- Look at the 'House for sale' adverts. Identify language features in terms of (1) headings ('Luxury villa for sale'), (2) appropriate words/phrases ('ideal for entertaining'), (3) picture (what is shown). Compare these with modern equivalents. Take one of the houses advertised in *The Egyptian News* and re-advertise it as if it was being sold today.

- Use the time line at the end of the book. Select an entry upon the line and find further information (from this book or others) that could be added to the line (e.g. 1279–1213 BC Rameses II rules Egypt. Then add 'He was responsible for building more temples than any other pharaoh').

- Look at selected extracts from texts that show how authors make effective use of background information (e.g. Sutcliff/ Fyson, etc.) to provide the setting for a story based on that period of time. Using information from *The Egyptian News*, create the beginning for a suitable novel for children.

HEADLINE NEWS

Find six news stories in *The Egyptian News*.

Write down the headline. Make some notes about the story.

Devise a different headline that could go with this story.

Headlines in book	The story is about	alternative headline

TOP GODS

Cut out the rectangles below. Match the gods to their description. Use page 17 to help you.

Wife of Osiris, mother of Horus

God whose symbol is a magic eye

The god of embalming

King of the gods, protector of Pharaoh

The god of the dead

Goddess of birth

6 Exploring feelings

Children enjoy hearing about someone very much like themselves. They love tales about boys and girls . . . who have moods and get angry as they do, who are sometimes naughty and get into trouble but who, in the end, receive the reassurance of being loved and wanted. They enjoy sharing the experiences and emotions which a well-written story triggers and willingly project into it their own feelings of fear, insecurity, anger, joy and relief.

(Phinn 1992 pp. 48–9)

In one way or another, all good stories help us to reflect on our feelings and emotions. Stories often help young children to find a language to express their hopes and fears and provide good opportunities for discussing their experience. It is salutary to remind ourselves that for some children separation and loss are very much a part of their lives. For others, commonplace worries like a fear of the dark may yet be quite disturbing. In working with texts we must be careful that we are not too preoccupied with our own agendas and objectives. We must allow the space for children to map the lessons that good texts teach onto their own developing experience. Because this is an area in which individual response is more important than literacy teaching, we have only selected a limited number of texts for this chapter – although many more could join them.

Exploring feelings can cover a vast range. Here are a few suggestions that tie into books we use in other chapters:

- enjoyment and happiness (e.g. *One Smiling Grandma*);
- family relationships (e.g. *Zoo*);
- love, hate and jealousy (e.g. *Snow White in New York*);
- separation and conflict (e.g. *Always Adam*);
- surprise (e.g. *Handa's Surprise*);
- social prejudice (e.g. *Voices in the Park*).

The titles in this chapter

Jez Alborough	*Where's my Teddy?*
Martin Waddell and Patrick Benson	*Owl Babies*
Martin Waddell and Barbara Firth	*Can't You Sleep, Little Bear?*
Dyan Sheldon and Gary Blythe	*The Whales' Song*

Where's My Teddy?

Written and illustrated by Jez Alborough.

Walker Books ISBN 0-744-53058

Range: stories with predictable structures and patterned language.

Themes: fear; loss; security.

Terminology: rhymes; cover; title; page; story; onset; rime; phoneme.

Outline

Eddy loses his teddy in the woods. As he seeks it, he encounters a huge bear, who has also lost a teddy.

Ways of working

Text

Cover features

Look at all the different things that are on the cover of a book, particularly:

- the title;
- the picture;
- the blurb on the back;
- the review notes.

Introduce the children to these terms and familiarise them with examples on the cover of the book. Read these and then, with the children's suggestions, compile a list of 'things we learned from the cover'. This could be tried with the covers of other books.

Context cues

Go through the text, placing paper or post-it notes over the nouns used. Ask the children to read it with you and, when they come to a covered word, suggest what it could be. Collect two suggestions and, for each of these, ask the children why they think their chosen word is the right one for the space.

The woods

Looking on the inside of the cover, find the double page spread showing the path going into the woods. Ask the children what might be along this path and make a list of their suggestions.

Individual actions

As a piece of dramatic role play, ask the children to re-enact Eddy's actions from the text in sequence, up to the point where he sees the Big Bear, e.g. tip-toeing through the forest, hearing gigantic footsteps. Repeat some of the best actions and ask the children how Eddy would have felt as he undertook them.

Dialogue pairs

Working in pairs, ask the children to try saying the lines Eddy and the giant teddy speak on meeting each other. Could they think of a different four-line exchange for Eddy and the Bear? For example, could they do one that begins with Eddy saying 'Who are you?'

Developing story structures

Ask children to identify the beginning of the story, the middle and the end. Can they place key events in sequence on a 'story ladder'? To do this they draw a ladder consisting of three steps. On each rung, the children draw key events of the story in sequence. Ask the children to focus on particular events, e.g. when Eddy is confronted with the giant teddy. Once they have tried a ladder for this text ask them to try one other for another story they know.

Sentence

Reorder some of the sentences, e.g. 'teddy my want I!' Write each word onto a piece of card and either place these on the carpet and ask children to slide them back into order or ask individual children to each come and hold a card. The rest of the class then have to tell this row of children where they should move to make a sentence that makes sense.

Extension

- Ask the children to try to retell the story from the point of view of teddy bears. Did they feel frightened when they lost their owners? What did they think when they were found? Children can do additional pictures for the book, showing one of the teddies. Text can be added explaining how the teddy felt after the ordeal.
- Write a letter from Eddy to the Big Bear asking him or her to become friends. The other half of the class can do the other side of the exchange and write from the Big Bear to Eddy. Encourage the children to write back. The correspondence could

> **Word notes**
>
> Can the children identify the rhyming words in the text? Make a list of words that have rhyming partners in the book. Put this on display and, as you read through the text, ask children if they can find words to match up with the rhyming partners you have listed.
>
> Make a book shaped as a teddy for each letter of the alphabet. Give each teddy a name which begins with a letter. These can then be hung on a wall. Children can then add words (pictures from magazines, etc.) which start with the same letter as the teddy's name, e.g. Freddy the Teddy has a fish, flower, fridge; Henna the Teddy has a hat, hammer, house; and so on.

then be continued over time.
- Ask the children to think of their own experiences of losing toys. Can they think of a time when they lost a particular favourite? Is it still lost?
- Take a trip to the woods. Find a park or woodland that can be reached by bus and take a journey there. Children could bring their teddies along.

Links to other texts

Read other books in which children lose treasured objects, e.g. Shirley Hughes's *Dogger*.

TEDDY OPPOSITES

Cut out the teddies.
Match the opposites and stick them down on a sheet of paper.

© Merchant & Thomas 1999, Picture Books for the Literacy Hour.

LOST! FREDDY THE TEDDY!

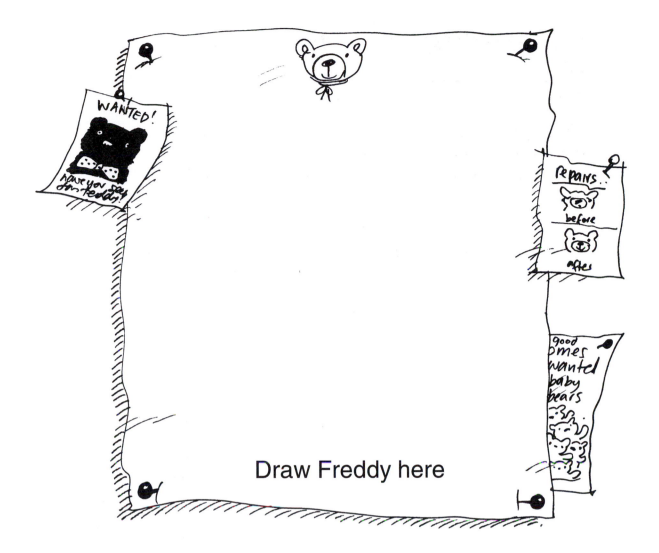

Draw Freddy here

Description of Freddy:

Last seen:

If you find Freddy, return him to:

Owl Babies

Written by Martin Waddell and illustrated by Patrick Benson.

Walker Books ISBN 0-744-53167-5

Learning opportunities

Range: stories by significant children's authors; stories that raise issues.

Themes: character's feelings; speech representation; points of view of different characters.

Terminology: speech; feeling; character; setting.

Outline

Three owl babies are left in their nest while their mother seeks their food. They express their feelings of uncertainty and nervousness until, after they wish for her, mum returns.

Ways of working

Text

Character types from speech
The three main ways in which a reader forms impressions of characters is through the things they do, their appearance and the things they say. *Owl Babies* provides an interesting example of the latter; in this story, the three owls look the same and undertake the same action (sitting in the tree), but the things they say build up a different picture of each owl. Point this out to the children. As the three owls speculate on where their mummy has gone and what might have happened, there is a pattern to the speech of each character. This activity can be developed through splitting the class into three groups and asking each group to read the speech of one of the owls and try to imagine what that owl is thinking and feeling. They could use their understanding of the three characters to try imagining how they would each respond to other situations, such as learning to fly, making a new nest and finding their own food.

Changing feelings
By following the words Sarah says through the book, children can follow the way in which the owls veer from anxiety to putting a brave face on their situation. They can consider each page and decide whether the owls are getting more nervous as the story progresses. One way of doing this is to draw a line on a piece of paper and label the two ends 'Beginning' and 'Ending'. These correspond to the beginning and end of the story. Along this line children can plot the way in which they think the three characters' feelings are progressing through the story. It may be worth noting that, up until the return of their mummy, the owl babies remain very still, a natural response to being in a scary and dark context. This changes dramatically when she returns ('they flapped and they danced, they bounced up and down').

Dig deeper into feelings
As they look at speech, children should consider what they think the owls are

really feeling. They may want to speculate on why Sarah suggests they should move closer together. They can also look at the last page, where the owls present a confident front to their mummy and discuss whether that's true of how they really felt. As they read the story you may want them to try and verbalise or jot down their speculations on what thoughts may have really been going through the owls' minds.

Sentence

Punctuation: *Owl Babies* presents a rich and imaginative text that uses a full range of punctuation marks. You can make the most of this opportunity to develop children's awareness of punctuation in a lively context! Particular examples include:

- parenthesis: the insertion of the little notes about owls thinking a lot;
- exclamation marks: Percy's speech provides an excellent example of the use of an exclamation mark in context – and is perfect for his frantic speech;
- italicised and capitalised text: the use of certain lettering styles for emphasis (for example, 'The baby owls *thought*' and 'AND SHE CAME').

The use of speech throughout the book also provides examples of speech marking. There is the potential for children to practise the demarcation of speech by writing an extra few pages about the babies, wait for their mother, producing their own three lines of speech modelled on the patterns followed in the book.

This means that, as well as being a brilliant story the book provides a resource of examples of the uses of the full range of punctuation marks in a real context. This can be particularly useful if displaying the poster version of the book (available from

Walker Books) in your classroom. You can also ask children to look at the use of a particular type of punctuation mark, such as brackets or inverted commas, and figure out what function they perform by looking at this story.

> **Word notes**
>
> The book provides an opportunity for looking at the way spellings of verbs can change quite dramatically as they go from present to past tense. The repetition of scenes where the owls 'thought' and the reminder that all owls 'think' a lot provide an opportunity to look at verbs with the 'ought' string of letters (bought, thought, sought, caught) and their present tense forms.
>
> The title provides an opportunity to look at the pluralisation of nouns ending in 'y' and find other examples of plurals with the '-ies' ending (e.g. cherries, ladies).

Extension

- Family responses: Ask the children to think how a trio made up of their own friends and family would respond differently to various situations. They could think of various scary or exciting times when they have reacted differently to a sibling or friend (e.g. how would different children react to a ride on a rollercoaster?).
- Night art: *Owl Babies* provides some excellent examples of night time scenes represented in pictures. Children could use it as a stimulus to their own night pictures. They could use coloured chalks on dark purple paper.

Links to other texts

The Owl Who Was Afraid of the Dark by Jill Tomlinson.

SARAH, PERCY AND BILL

Each set of speech bubbles shows what Sarah, Percy and Bill said at different times in the story. Can you fill in the empty bubbles?

OWL BABIES SEQUENCE

Cut out the rectangles and arrange them in the order in which they happened in the story.

The baby owls wished their mother would come.

They had to be brave, for things moved all around them.

They all sat on the same branch.

The baby owls came out of their house.

They sat on separate branches.

Their owl mother came.

The babies flapped and danced and bounced up and down.

The baby owls woke up.

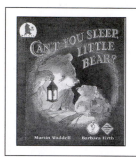

Can't You Sleep, Little Bear?

Written by Martin Waddell and illustrated by Barbara Firth.

Walker Books ISBN 0-744-51316-2

Learning opportunities

Range: stories with predictable and repetitive patterns; stories with familiar settings; significant authors.

Themes: fear of the dark; security.

Terminology: character; author; illustrator; blurb; full stop; question mark; speech marks; sentence; capital letter.

Outline

It is night in the cosy cave where Big Bear and Little Bear live. Little Bear is in bed but cannot sleep because it is too dark and he repeatedly interrupts Big Bear, who is trying to read a book by the fire. Big Bear patiently tries to coax Little Bear to go to sleep.

Ways of working

Text

Designing a book cave
Before doing this activity you need to make sure the children cannot see the blurb on the back of *Can't You Sleep, Little Bear?* Identify the basic features of a book cover and produce a diagram of the way they are laid out – author name, illustrator, title, publisher. Ask the children to search for blurbs on picture books in the classroom and produce your own examples for discussion. After

reading it, the children then produce their own blurb for *Can't You Sleep, Little Bear?* and compare their version with the actual one on the book.

Little Bear's diary
Provide a model of a diary to show the layout and purpose and ask the children to complete the diary from Little Bear's perspective. They will need to consider Little Bear's fear of the dark, what effect the different lanterns have on him and the ways in which Big Bear tries to comfort him; then, writing in the first person, they can imagine it is the day after the events in the story and record Little Bear's account of the events.

Similar experiences
The book provides a starting point for children to explore the two elements of the things that they are or have been frightened by and the ways in which their fears can be allayed. In particular, they can look at the way in which shapes and sounds in the night can seem more frightening than they actually are. They can also reflect upon their own experiences of disturbing someone who has put them to bed. Babysitters can provide good raw material for this.

Dialogue
The story is divided up into exchanges between Big Bear and Little Bear. When these take place, from the opening line 'Can't you sleep, Little Bear?' there is an exchange that is the same on each

occasion, leading to Little Bear's words 'The dark all around us'. Children can learn this dialogue and, splitting into pairs, each take one of the parts in this exchange. It can be used as a model for script writing, and children can place the style of speech in brackets, e.g.

Big Bear (annoyed): Can't you sleep, Little Bear?

Children can then try creating similar exchanges of their own, with varied opening lines such as:

'Eat your dinner, Little Bear' or 'Where are my wellies, Big Bear?'

Sentence

Encourage the children to make speech balloons from blank post-its and match these to the illustrations in the book. These can be directly from the text or ones that the children compose themselves.

Question marks
Type out the section starting on the third page, that begins 'Can't you sleep, Little Bear?', deleting the question marks. Ask the children to insert these and to check their efforts with the original text.

Extension

- Big Bear questions: children can make a list of the sorts of questions adults ask children in their care, a classic example being 'Can't you sleep?' They can compile these on a list and might be able to use some of them as a stimulus for their own Little Bear and Big Bear story.
- Night time: children can think of their own experiences of being outside at night and make notes on these,

Word notes

Vocabulary that conveys a feeling of security and warmth is evident throughout the story – settled, cuddling, cosy, warm, safe. Encourage the children to find words to describe particular settings, drawing on the story (e.g. a cosy cave, the woods at night).

The names of the characters have capital letters – Baby Bear and Big Bear. Ask the children to search for the names of other characters in other stories available in the classroom and get them to write these on a large sheet of paper, ensuring that the names begin with a capital letter.

working through their senses asking 'What would you see?', 'What would you hear?' These could be used to write a piece of poetry about the experience of being outside in the night.
- Look at the pictures and describe the expression of the characters in each of them (e.g. 'happy', 'interested', 'engrossed'). Children could try looking at the way in which the depiction of eyes, mouths and stances is used to indicate the feelings of characters.

Links to other texts

Jill Tomlinson's *The Owl Who Was Afraid of the Dark* looks at the same issue, as does *Scare Yourself to Sleep* and *The Ankle Grabber*. You could also introduce children to Martin Waddell's *Let's Go Home, Little Bear*. Joanna Harrison's *Dear Bear* and *Bear under the Stairs* also use bears to look at irrational fears.

SCARED OF THE DARK

Why do we get scared in the dark? Can you think of some of the scary things that keep us awake at night?

DIALOGUE

Put these things characters say in the order in which they appear in the story. Cut out the bubbles and stick them down in order:

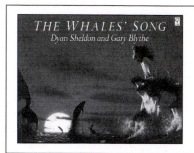

The Whales' Song

Written by Dyan Sheldon and illustrated by Gary Blythe.

Red Fox ISBN 0-099-26349-1

Learning opportunities

Range: stories with familiar settings; persuasive texts.
Themes: nature; conservation; mystery; folk-lore; magic.
Terminology: point of view; opinion; debate; imagery.

Outline

Lily listens to her grandmother's tales of encounters with whales and, despite the discouragement of her uncle, experiences her own 'whales' song'.

Ways of working

Text

Contrasting characters
Reading through the text, explore the three main characters in the book using information from both text and illustrations – how is their character presented orally and visually? What relationship is depicted between them? Ask children to work in small groups of two and three and to write the names of the three main characters on pieces of paper. They then place these face downwards and, selecting two of the names, list the similarities and differences between them. They do this until they have tried three different combinations of character pairs.

Point of view
The story is told very much from Lily's point of view. This can be seen in the way her dreams and the faint things she hears are recounted. How would the story have read from the point of view of one of the other characters? Children can try retelling the story, either as Uncle Frederick or as Grandmother.

Ask the children to find the two opinions about whales represented in the text – as creatures of beauty and as useful objects. Explore these viewpoints and discuss which they think is true.

Setting
It is not clear from the story where or when it is set but, looking at the illustrations, children can try finding clues as to whether it is a modern story or set in the past. The story centres on one small setting, a house by the sea with a jetty. Children can draw a map of the setting and then describe the various parts of it.

Past and future
The story makes interesting use of time, with characters recalling the past. Children can fill in other details about the time around this story. Why, for example, is Lily staying with Grandmother? What might happen to Lily in the future – to whom will she recount her 'whales' story'. Children can make a list of story guesses –

things they are not told in the story but that they guess. These do not need to be backed up by information in the text, such as why Uncle Frederick is so cross and what happened after the ending of the story. Children can feel free to speculate.

Sentence

The children could focus on speech and speech marks within the story. Speech could be taken out of the text and written as a play script in shared writing activity. As they look at some of the story guesses, described above, children could consider some of the conversations that could arise as, for example, Lily tells Grandma about the whales' singing. These could be written using the appropriate punctuation.

Word notes

Synonyms: Collect all the words from the text which mean 'to say' and discuss the mood each implies. Ask children to try finding other examples from other texts or from a thesaurus and build up a comprehensive list of speech words. When they write their own conversations (see 'sentence level activities') children could use some of these words instead of 'said'.

Extension

- Use this as an opportunity for oral story telling – imagine you are Lily now grown up and retell the story describing the events that happened. How would Lily explain what happened? Don't forget to include details garnered from the story, such as the attitude of Uncle Frederick and the amount of time spent waiting on the jetty.
- Use hot-seating as a way of exploring the three main characters. To do this, individual children take on the personality of a particular character from the story and the rest of the class decide what questions they want to ask them and the children must answer (in character) questions posed.
- Write to Greenpeace/Friends of the Earth to find out more about whales or other key conservation issues. Make a presentation of the information to the whole school or another class.

Links to other texts

Dear Greenpeace by Simon James provides a contrasting tale of a girl and a whale.
The Garden, also by Sheldon and Blythe, allows you to look at visual style and themes.

TIME LINE

Cut out the events and sort them into the order in which they happened.

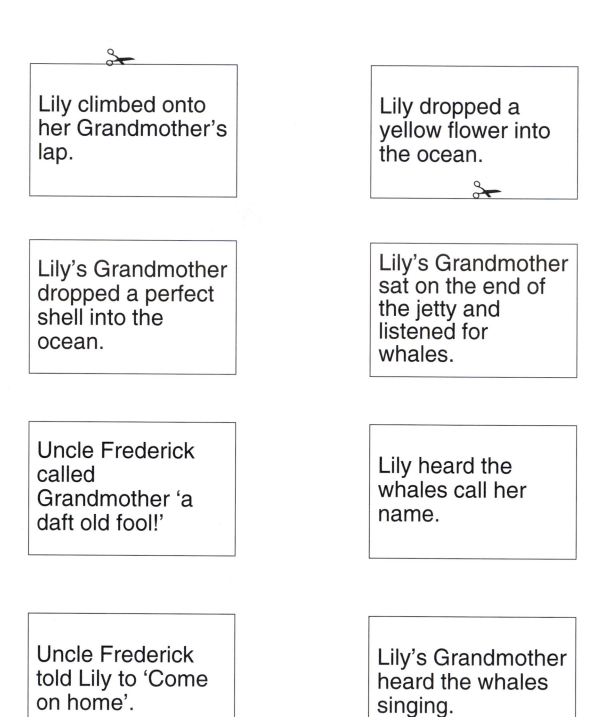

Lily climbed onto her Grandmother's lap.

Lily dropped a yellow flower into the ocean.

Lily's Grandmother dropped a perfect shell into the ocean.

Lily's Grandmother sat on the end of the jetty and listened for whales.

Uncle Frederick called Grandmother 'a daft old fool!'

Lily heard the whales call her name.

Uncle Frederick told Lily to 'Come on home'.

Lily's Grandmother heard the whales singing.

WHALE THOUGHTS

Write some notes showing what the characters in *The Whales' Song* think and feel.

What does Grandma think

What does Uncle Frederick think

What does Lily think

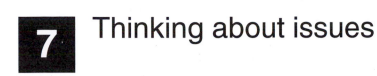

7 Thinking about issues

As all of us who work with children and books are aware, there is a power to the written word which can lend additional authority or affirmation to themes (such as bullying) being discussed or worked on elsewhere, either in the classroom or in the internal world of an individual. In the broadest sense, literature can be and is used for the purpose of self-help or personal growth in both arenas.

(Stones 1998, p. 5)

This chapter looks at the power of story in raising social issues. Many of the themes addressed are cross-curricular, lending themselves particularly to the exploration of moral issues and personal and social education. The picture books we have worked with provide plenty of useful material for literacy work. If they are being used within the Literacy Hour, teachers will need to make sure that some of the follow-up activities are also planned in. This may involve extending your study of these titles outside the Literacy Hour.

Like all of the other categories we have used in this book, 'thinking about issues' is wide-ranging. Some examples of issues that you can raise through reading picture books are:

- alienation and social exclusion;
- bullying;
- health education;
- power and domination;
- cooperation and conflict;
- racism;
- animal rights;
- gender roles.

The titles in this chapter

Martin Waddell and Helen Oxenbury	*Farmer Duck*
Babette Cole	*Dr Dog*
Kathryn Cave and Chris Riddell	*Something Else*
Anthony Browne	*Zoo*

Farmer Duck

Written by Martin Waddell and illustrated by Helen Oxenbury.

Walker Books ISBN 0-744-53660

Learning opportunities

Range: stories with predictable and patterned language.

Themes: cruelty; cooperation.

Terminology: character; dialogue; sequence; sentence; full stop; upper case.

Outline

The book is a moral tale that focuses on the cruel treatment of a duck by a farmer. It contains a number of interesting features. The animals in the book have a meeting which is reported, but the animals' discussion takes place in animal sounds ('moo', 'baa', 'cluck').

Ways of working

Text

Discussing characters

Discuss the character of the farmer with the children. Ask them to imagine they once stayed on the farm and then get them to write their recollections of what the farmer looked like and the sorts of things he said and did.

Ask the children if they can think of any other cruel characters in stories. Discuss the differences and similarities between them. Make a list of these.

Ask children to create a list of books in which the bad characters are chased away or destroyed and the other characters live happily ever after.

Dialogue

Imagine a conversation between the farmer and the duck. The duck is trying to tell the farmer that he is working him too hard but the farmer does not agree. Discuss how the characters can be portrayed through the dialogue by making two lists, one collecting the sorts of things the duck would say as he pleads with the farmer and the other listing the sort of cruel things the farmer would say to the duck. In brackets alongside these, ask the children to come up with an adverb like the speech directions in a play (e.g. 'sadly' 'angrily'), showing what manner they think these speakers would adopt as they say their various lines. They can use these lines as a resource to be drawn on as they attempt to write a script for the conversation. They can also produce a play script that is based on the animals' meeting in the barn, translating the animal sounds! They can then role-play the parts as they re-enact the scene.

Retell the story

Ask the children to identify key points in the plot on a story map. To do this they need to draw a line on a piece of paper along which they plot the major events in this story. Before undertaking this, it's worth trying a couple of well-known examples on the board. They can then have a go at mapping *Farmer Duck* and can then use this diagram to retell the story orally.

Farmyard map

Ask the children to draw a map of the farmyard, pointing out the different buildings and places where Farmer Duck did his chores. Once they have done this, ask them to add notes to the map, showing where certain significant events took place (e.g. where did the animals hold their meeting?).

Identify and compare story elements

Ask the children to find other stories which begin in a similar vein to *Farmer Duck*, i.e. 'There once was . . .'. What sort of ending would they expect to a story opening sentence like this? The beginning of this story outlines the character of the 'villain' of the piece straight away. Ask the children if they can identify any other stories which do this. In contrast, can they identify stories in which the 'villain' appears later?

Ask the children to identify the main features of the ending of the book, e.g. the villain is chased away and the other characters are happy. The children can then find other stories which have similar endings.

Sentence

Blu tac paper slips over the verbs in the text and ask the children to think of words that would make sense each time they encounter one of these spaces, e.g. 'The duck ...... the cow from the field'. This can be tied to work on verbs used in the book, e.g. stole/creaked/wriggled. As they encounter these gaps, make a list of the words they think could fit into each space. Ask them why they think their suggestions belong there. In some cases the answer will be that they have been led by the picture, in others it may be some feature of the story that has guided them.

Focus on identifying full stops. Emphasise their use in reading aloud. Read aloud a passage and ask children to stop you when they think there is a break between sentences.

Extension

- What were the rules of the farm collective? Write them out on a poster. To do this children could try imagining different rules that would be contributed

Word notes

Discuss word meanings, e.g. 'They creaked up the stairs'. What does 'creaked' mean? Can the children think of other noises which may be made when moving about? Can they change them into verbs, e.g. 'They whooshed out of the door'?

As they read through the text, ask the children to list the words that end in 'ck' which feature in the book, e.g. duck/cluck/quack/luck/rock/back. Ask the children to make a sentence which contains as many of these words as possible while still maintaining sense, e.g. 'The duck threw a rock and heard a cluck and a quack'.

by or because of specific animals (e.g. 'No crowing before sunrise').

- Children can write to the Royal Society for the Prevention of Cruelty to Animals or other animal welfare organisations, asking for information about how they tackle the mistreatment of animals.
- Write the story from the farmer's viewpoint. This could take the form of an apology letter from the repentant farmer to the animals, apologising for and explaining his behaviour.
- Write an article for the local *Farmers' Journal*, describing the events on the farm.
- Write the sequel to the story – will the duck become like the farmer? Will the farmer return?

Links to other texts

Draw upon children's experience of other stories with cruel characters, e.g. *101 Dalmations, Snow White*. They may have read these or seen films of the stories.

ANIMAL VOICES

Look at the animal meeting in *Farmer Duck*. Fill in these voice bubbles to translate their animal noises into English.

NEWS STORY

Imagine you are a reporter for a newspaper. You are sent to report on events at Farmer Duck's farm.

Who would you talk to?

What would the farmer say?

Write your notes here ➡

Now write your news story. Give it a headline and picture.

Headline

Picture

Dr Dog

Written and illustrated by Babette Cole.

Red Fox ISBN 0-099-65081-9

Learning opportunities

Range: humorous stories; information texts; explanations.
Themes: health; diet.
Terminology: diagram; informal language; technical language.

Outline

Dr Dog is the pet of an unhealthy family. He has to solve their ailments, explaining their causes and giving advice. The straightforward explanations he offers of wind and worms make this text a hit with children.

Ways of working

Text

Health problems
Before reading the story, explain to the children that they are about to read a book about a seriously unhealthy family. Ask them to make a list of the sorts of problems people can incur when they don't take care of themselves. List these. As a prompt you might want to tell them that the family includes a teenager and a baby, etc. Keep the list and, on reading the book, check to see how many suggested ailments were predicted by the class.

Describing the Gumboyles
Looking at the Gumboyle family, ask children to produce a description of them. This could take the form of a drama activity in which children form pairs, one playing the part of Dr Dog and the other playing the part of the colleague who advises him to take a holiday at the end of the book. Focus on some of the features of the text that will help children to compile their moans about the family. Obviously there are their health problems but you could also point out the blasé attitude they adopt to, for example, Fiona Gumboyle's dizziness.

Look at slogans
Collect the examples of the slogans, the short and pithy pieces of advice with which Dr Dog ends his consultations with each patient. Can children think of other examples from road safety advice or public information adverts? Discuss what makes a good slogan; for example, does rhyme help (certainly children tend to remember the rhyming one in this book)? Look at the length of slogans, then, thinking of some other pieces of advice they would want to give, ask children to devise their own. These could be about safety issues in school or around railway tracks, poolside safety in the swimming baths or safety in the kitchen. Encourage the use of rhyme and pithy phrases.

Advice
Look at the advice Dr Dog gives and the way it is presented in the text. Compare and contrast the 'normal illustrations' with the diagrams used, considering the value of diagrams in this text. How have they been labelled? What other types of text might we find them in?

Health information
Look at the purpose of health information. Alongside looking at this text, select a range of health education leaflets, available at a pharmacy, and discuss the purpose and audience of such advice. Ask children to weigh up the degree to which they promote positive behaviour (the 'do's') and discourage negative habits (the 'don'ts'). Keep this balance in mind when reading

through Dr Dog and consider what the needs of his audience were and the extent to which they needed a firm 'Don't!' Compare the presentation of information in the leaflets with the words of Dr Dog. Is he more or less formal?

Sentence

This text provides an ideal opportunity to focus on the imperative verb.

The text provides a resource for looking at verbs. List the verbs used in the text, there being a wide and crude range to draw upon! Note the use of the imperative verb in the advice Dr Dog gives: 'Never scratch . . .', 'Never swap . . .'.

Point out the use of the exclamation mark to end these instructions. These points can link with the above idea of children devising their own slogans.

The text also provides an interesting stimulus for looking at standard and non-standard English. Children can look at some of the regional and colloquial expressions used for problems such as wind or nits. This can lead to looking at other health matters, such as being sick, where a range of regional and non-standard terms proliferate (such as the recent addition to English of the American term 'barf').

Extension

- Design posters/leaflets dealing with particular health issues and aimed at a specific audience, such as younger children in the school. Consider what information will go on the poster and the slogan that will be used to communicate the main points. As they do this children should look at the contrast between Dr Dog's technical and down-to-earth explanations, deciding which they will opt for.
- Design a radio or television commercial to persuade people to adopt a more healthy lifestyle (a study

> ### Word notes
>
> The text shows an interesting use of technical vocabulary alongside less technical explanations. Make a list of some of the health terms, such as 'nits', 'wind' and 'worms', and ask children to write their own short definitions of these problems, possibly drawing on other sources of information. Ask them to try producing their definition within ten words. Then try and shorten it to eight or six. As they do this they should note the words that get removed and the ones that are kept.

of radio and television commercials linked to health can provide a good starting point). Again, the slogan can be used here.

- Involve the school nurse, doctor or other support services from the local community. Ask them to come and discuss key health issues with the children, e.g. asthma, or to talk about their work. Alternatively, use their visit as an opportunity for the children to interview the health visitor (this would need to be planned by the class teacher).
- Get the children to study some examples of problems related to health issues from the problem pages of magazines (you will need to select these carefully). Discuss with the children the problems and the advice given. Use sample letters for the children to provide replies. Role-play in which one child gives advice to another on an imaginary problem can extend this activity further and provide a good opportunity for considering oral skills and communication.

Links to other texts

This text links well with non-fiction texts about the body and health, such as *How Your Body Works* (Usborne).

APOSTROPHE DOCTOR

An apostrophe shows one thing belongs to another, e.g. "Chloe's boat" – the 's shows the boat is Chloe's.

Match the characters to their problems and list them using 's.

For example if ⎡Dr Dog⎤ matches ⎡worms⎤

List it as *Dr Dog's worms*.

family ──────────────────────
```
                Kurt Gumboyle
Gerty Gumboyle        Dr Dog
Kev Gumboyle  Tim Gumboyle
Baby Gumboyle
Grandpa Gumboyle
```

──────────────── problem
```
  Wind
          lungs
    ears        nits

           stress
  worms          tonsils
```

1 _____

2 _____

3 _____

4 _____

5 _____

6 _____

7 _____

DR YOU

Imagine you are Doctor for a family with lots of problems, such as:

rotting teeth

smelly armpits

lost voices

dirty fingernails

sweaty feet

Write your Doctor notes for them giving them names. Note down their problems and your cure.

DOG HEALTH CLINIC

Patients name _____

Problem _____

_____

_____

Cure _____

_____

_____

DOG HEALTH CLINIC

Patients name _____

Problem _____

_____

_____

Cure _____

_____

_____

DOG HEALTH CLINIC

Patients name _____

Problem _____

_____

_____

Cure _____

_____

_____

DOG HEALTH CLINIC

Patients name _____

Problem _____

_____

_____

Cure _____

_____

_____

Something Else

Written by Kathryn Cave and illustrated by Chris Riddell.

Puffin ISBN 0-140-54907-2

Learning opportunities

Range: stories/short novels that raise issues, e.g. bullying, bereavement, injustice.

Themes: friendship and alienation, the differences between characters and their attitudes to one another.

Terminology: feeling; point of view; character; opinion.

Outline

Something Else has no friends. The other creatures spurn his attempts to befriend them. Then Something turns up and their relationship develops from a rocky beginning into friendship.

Ways of working

Text

Raising issues about alienation
Something Else provides an excellent starting point for children to gather thoughts about the issues raised in a story and their response to them. Children can identify social, moral and cultural issues in the story by looking at the name 'Something Else'. You can ask them why he is called that, and how is he different from the other creatures. They can also look at the differences among the other characters. Are they really such a homogeneous grouping? As they read the story children could look in the text and pictures for the prejudices that cause the others to alienate Something Else.

Ask children to look at how the illustrations build up this feeling of loneliness. They can compare the two pages where Something Else 'did his best to be like the others' with the parallel events on the 'It was no good' pages.

The first page
The structure of the lines on the first page can be used to prompt discussion. The story begins with one sentence.

The layout of this sentence is significant. Ask children why the line breaks occur where they do. Why isn't this sentence written as one long line? What distinct fact do we learn on each line? Children should then devise their own opening line layout. Ask them to look at the facts and feelings that they would want to express in the opening of a story. Then ask them to plan the opening of a story scanning a few lines, with something distinct communicated in each line. Encourage them to experiment with the line layout and page positioning as they create their own story opening.

Unfamiliar world
There are no human characters in this story until the last two pages. The world these creatures inhabit is different. Children can look at features of landscape and activity to see what is different about this setting. Ask children to look at Something Else's house. Children can describe the setting and consider what sort of a response it evokes. They can compare it with the homes of other characters in fiction (such as Charlie's poor but loving home in *Charlie and the Chocolate Factory* by Roald Dahl).

Character's point of view
As the narrative in *Something Else* develops we can focus attention on how things look and feel from the 'point of view' of a particular character. Children can create a diary noting how their overall impression of Something Else is built up, page by page. They can note his actions, his expressions and his experiences and record their own feelings about the character. They can also look at how these feelings develop through the opening pages and from the point at which Something strolls into his house.

Tracking a relationship
Look at the relationship that develops between Something Else and Something

(the creature who visits him). These can be tracked in diagram form along parallel lines, noticing how the bubbliness of one is met by the outrage of the other, the sadness of Something matched by Something Else's understanding of what he must do. Track the relationship, from one picture to the next looking at words and expressions to see how these two characters are reacting and feeling.

Naming

Naming is an interesting feature of stories. It influences the way in which the reader views a character. If he is called 'Uncle Mike' a character feels different from if he is called 'the crook'. Look at the terms used to denote characters in this story, particularly 'the creature' who visits Something Else. He moves from being called 'Something' to 'the creature' to 'Something to be friends with'. What does this tell us about how he is viewed in the story? Children can also look at the names and nicknames of characters and what they tell us about them. Examples can range from 'Uriah Heep' to 'The Wild Things' and on to 'Batman'.

The others

The point of view of the other characters who isolate Something Else is also interesting. Children can explore this by working in two's and role-playing the parts of two of these other characters. What is their point of view in the story? At various times what do they think and feel? Children can try and imagine what sort of relationship these other characters have among themselves. This could lead to story writing about one of the other creatures in the illustrations.

Sentence

Throughout the book there are engaging examples of the use of pronouns. From the opening encounters where 'He' (Something Else) approaches 'Them' (the other creatures) the play on pronouns becomes a notable feature of the book's language. Children can look at whom the pronouns refer to and track the relationships among the characters in terms of their pronouns, noting how, for example, Something Else moves from being an isolated 'he' who 'they' (the other characters) reject to being one of a 'they'

himself. Look at the pronoun used for the creature and for the boy who appears at the end. In many ways the story is summed up in the closing line: 'They moved right up and made room for him too'.

Word notes

Ask children to look at the '-thing' stem and list the words that end with it. They could also look at other stems such as '-one' and '-body'. These may inspire some story ideas of their own.

They could look at fictional and actual names. Throughout the book the words Something Else are capitalised (indicating that they denote a named individual). Children could look at origins of their own names.

Extension

- Look at how emotion is communicated through illustration: children can look in other books to see the ways in which the pictures express the feelings of the characters. In a book like *The Visitors Who Came to Stay*, the pictures of a contented home life degenerate into chaos, reflecting the anxiety of the central character as her family changes.
- Children could explore the feelings of isolation. Children can recall their own experiences of feeling left out of friendships. A poem like Roger McGough's 'First day at school' (in *You Tell Me* by Michael Rosen and Roger McGough) vividly expresses the feelings of a child on the fringes of a new school.
- Children could devise a comprehensive list of the ways in which friends can relate, looking at the conflicts that can occur, the jealousies, the good times, etc. Using a strip of paper folded into four frames children could devise and chart a developing friendship in four stages.
- This is a fantastic setting with odd characters, but children could look at the aspects of the story that are true to life. They could look at this aspect of other stories in which there are fantastic features but recognisable issues and experiences they can relate to.

COMPOUND WORDS

Something Else is full of words like 'something', 'nothing', etc.

Using the word beginnings and word endings below how many longer words can you make?

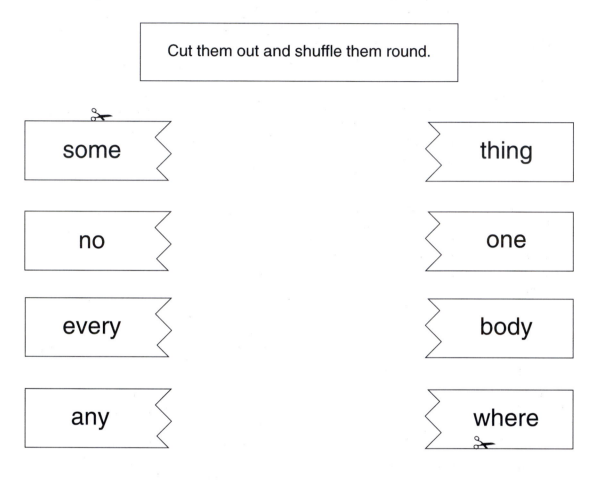

Cut them out and shuffle them round.

some

no

every

any

thing

one

body

where

Make a list of your new words.

THINKS BUBBLES

Fill in the bubbles to show how Something Else felt and what he thought at different times in the story.

When the new creature stuck out a paw and walked right in

When the new creature left Something Else's house

When the other creatures said 'You don't belong'

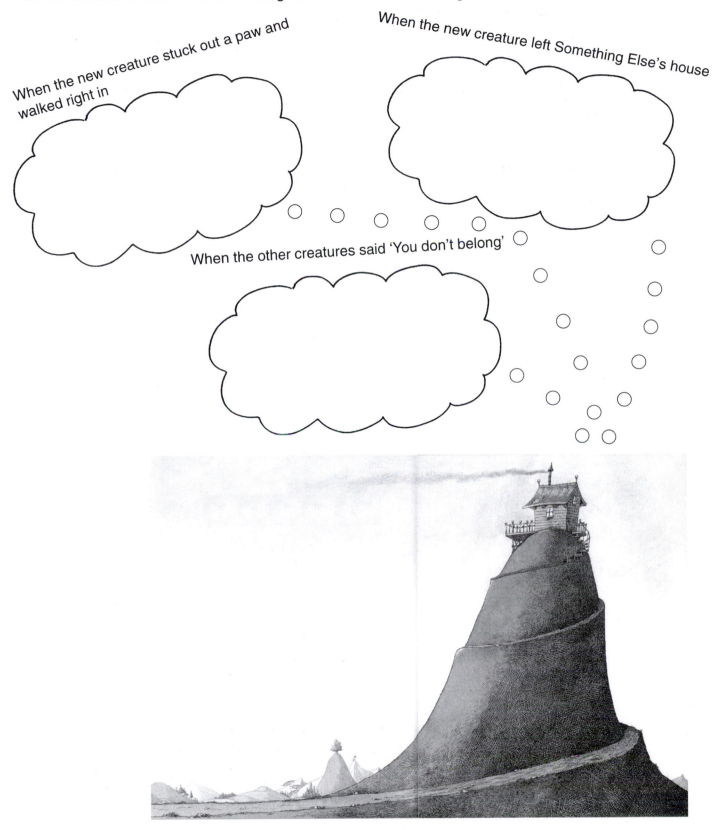

Illustration (page 2) by Chris Riddell from SOMETHING ELSE by Kathryn Cave, illustrated by Chris Riddell (Viking, 1994). Copyright © Chris Riddell, 1994. Reproduced by permission of Penguin Books Ltd.

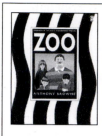

Zoo

Written and illustrated by Anthony Browne.

Red Fox ISBN 0-099-21901-8

Learning opportunities

Range: stories with familiar settings; stories by the same author.

Themes: family relationships; family outings; animals in captivity.

Terminology: narrative; narration and voice; setting.

Outline

This story follows a family on their day out to the zoo including the journey (they get stuck in a traffic jam) and one child's dream at the end of the day. The story is written from a child's point of view – the highlight of the day is the burger and chips – and invites us to reflect on family relationships and animals in captivity. Important parts of the story are told through the visual text.

Ways of working

Text

Representing characters' feelings
Children can read the book closely focusing on how the main characters (the family) feel about each other through the written text, dialogue and illustration. You can model this by discussing how dad interacts with the man in the ticket booth. Ask children to create their own version of the first page, writing about what the narrator ('me') thinks about

himself and the other members of the family. Anthony Browne uses some speech bubbles to represent dialogue. Ask children to suggest more using 'post-its'. Children can also experiment with thought bubbles. You could extend this into freeze-frame work in drama.

Animals in captivity
Anthony Browne uses bars, fences and walls in a variety of ways to accentuate the theme of captivity. Ask children to study the illustrations and list where these devices are used, making a note of what they suggest. They should be encouraged to explore these techniques in their own art and poster-designing work. Along with these images of captivity, Browne conveys feelings of boredom and futility. Partly this is achieved by the matter-of-fact style of narration and partly through the art work. Children can study the illustrations, focusing on how human characteristics are used to suggest the animals' emotions, and how humans are given animal attributes (the ticket booth scene provides an early illustration of this).

Author–illustrator's style
Anthony Browne has a particularly distinctive visual style. His books explore common themes of family life, gender roles and stereotypes. Bring together a collection of Browne's books. Encourage children to identify the key themes in each book. One way of

approaching these is to use sheets of A4 with two columns. In one column children write down what the story is about and where it is set. On the other side they write down what they learnt about from reading the book (include other titles like *Willy the Wimp*, *The Piggy Book*, *Gorilla* and *Voices in the Park*). Ask your children to find out more about Anthony Browne by writing to the publishers. Set up a critics' forum in your classroom in which children work in groups to decide upon and argue for their favourite title. This can then be put to the vote and the winning Anthony Browne story can be given the 'Class 4 Book Award'.

Sentence

Look at the way speech is reported in *Zoo*. Instead of 'said', the author uses a number of verbs that suggest animal behaviour (e.g. howl, whine, jeer). Study these by substituting different verbs and evaluating their effect. You could also get children to discuss the effects of the short, factual sentences that Anthony Browne uses: 'It was brilliant'; 'Two of them had a fight'; 'Miserable thing'. It is also worth looking at the effect of ending the story with a question.

Word notes

Dad's rather feeble jokes are puns – 'traffic jam' and 'hot dog'. Children can collect puns or read them from other sources (e.g. Janet and Allan Ahlberg's *The Ha Ha Bonk Book*).

Extension

- The book leads naturally into thinking about families and family roles and how we interact on holidays and outings.
- You can also discuss traditional stereotypes of mothers and fathers.

- Ask children to script and enact a 'wildlife documentary' on a family (either their own or an imaginary family).
- In discussing the 'human' characteristics of animals (or the way humans project characteristics onto animals) you could look at the Nick Parkes video *Creature Comforts*.
- Think about zoos and children's feelings about them.
- This could lead to writing to a zoo and asking about the problems of keeping animals in captivity and the danger for animals whose natural habitat is being destroyed.
- Use reference material to investigate animals under threat and animals in captivity.
- Children can write argument and persuasive pieces on animal welfare.
- Write to the World Wide Fund for Nature and other organisations for information.
- Make posters and information leaflets on animal rights.

Links to other texts

Anthony Browne is an influential illustrator. Make a collection of his work. Ask children to look closely at his illustrations and the exploration of animal themes (particularly gorillas), as well as his representation of families and gender roles. *Piggybook* is another, more direct exploration of tension in family life, whereas the themes of masculinity are explored in *Willy the Wimp*. There are numerous well-informed explorations of animal conservation themes in other picture books. John Burningham's *Oi! Get Off Our Train!* is particularly good and Peter Haswell's *It's Now or Never* is an extremely informative text set out as an animal conservation alphabet.

FEELINGS

- After their day at the zoo how does mum feel about her family, the animals, the boys, her day out etc?
- Write her feelings in the thought bubbles.

- Write down the story of the day as told by mum in her secret diary.

CAGED IN

● What did the animals do at the zoo? (Use the words and pictures to make notes in each box.)

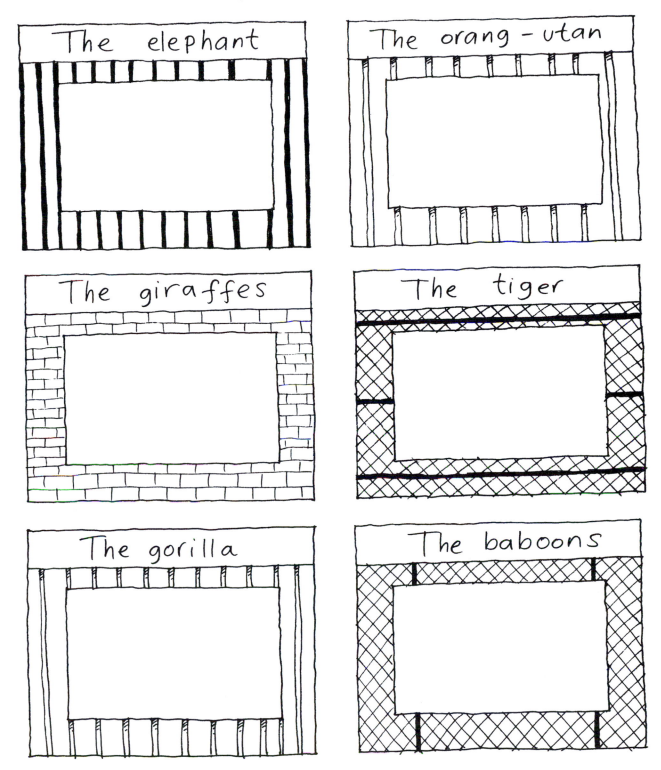

The elephant

The orang-utan

The giraffes

The tiger

The gorilla

The baboons

8 Building up resources

... picture storybooks, both those that are written for children and those that they create for themselves, provide the best material for learning to read and write, once they have discovered the pleasure of sharing a story read aloud and acquired sufficient confidence to begin to join in the actual reading. There are now sufficient picture storybooks of varying levels of difficulty to enable a whole programme to be based on books that children choose because they want to read them for themselves.

(Wells 1987, p.160)

In this chapter we look at ways of developing the school's stock of picture books. We begin by suggesting ways in which you can look critically at material before investing in it, and then go on to suggest a number of ways in which teachers can keep informed about the availability of new and established texts. Creating a collection of summaries like those produced in this book may be a useful way of sharing your ideas with colleagues, and planning how to use picture books in the Literacy Hour and elsewhere in the school curriculum. This is followed by guidance on how to develop text-related activities, such as the photocopiables that we have produced.

Critically evaluating picture books

Selecting picture books is certainly a difficult task. In choosing titles for this book we have had to make many omissions. There is no John Burningham, no Quentin Blake and no Peter Bailey, to mention but a few. But we had to stop somewhere. Teachers with a limited budget will be faced with similar constraints. Choices are made harder by the fact that personal preference tends to interact in a rather haphazard way with our criteria for selection. For example, we find that the work of Anthony Browne evokes rather variable responses in teacher colleagues. While most recognise the strength and talent in his work as a writer and illustrator, some will admit to 'just not liking his books'. This is, of course a classic example of how individual response to text can vary. Personal preference is unavoidable and it is probably quite appropriate to suggest that if you don't like a book yourself you're going to find it hard to inspire others with it. At the same time, we think it is important that we are not guided by personal choice alone.

Given the huge number of picture book titles that are published each year, and the importance of selecting appropriate material for children, we need to ask ourselves what we are looking for when purchasing material. As suggested above, it is often the case that one feature of the book outweighs all others. Nonetheless, the following list attempts to capture the essential features of a good picture book.

1. **The visual appeal of the book**. The most immediate impact of a picture book is likely to be through its visual features. Of course, it's not just a case of looking for images that are colourful and life-like. Some illustrators use a variety of techniques including pencil drawing, pastel shading, water colour and gouache. Their work may be influenced by other visual artists, painters or comic-strip illustrators. You will have your own preferences just as children will have theirs, but try to build up collections of work by those who have a distinctive style and those whose pictures add to the meanings of the printed word. Good quality illustrations help children to visualise the story and, in some cases, help children to come to terms with texts they might otherwise find quite challenging. The work of Marcia Williams, featured in this book, manages to do this very successfully. In a good picture book, written text works closely with images, and the clarity of print, its positioning on the page and the size and clarity of the font are important. Of course, when choosing big books for shared reading, it's important that the print size is large enough to be read at a distance.

2. **The interest level.** Even the most lavishly illustrated picture book with the most careful use of print features is doomed to failure if it is unable to capture the interest of child and adult readers. The book must be good enough to be read and reread and must be a subject worth exploring and a story worth telling. So, at one level or another it must relate to the interests and concerns of children. It must reflect or relate to children's lives. But since for much of the time, adults will be mediating the reading of these texts, they should also have the capacity to hold the adult's interest as well. Established author–illustrators such as Janet Ahlberg, Anthony Browne and Helen Oxenbury are able to make meaning at a number of levels, capturing the interest of child and adult readers simultaneously. Because they are able to do this, children are able to revisit their books seeing more subtleties each time they do.

3. **The book as a story.** To a certain extent this relates to the previous point. The story must be interesting and worth telling – but it should also be well told. The best picture books have well-developed characters, a clear sense of place and setting, and events, perhaps full of twists and surprises, that nonetheless constitute a narrative plot that holds our attention. Regardless of whether these elements are communicated through verbal or visual form, the story must work for us and our apprentice readers. In good picture books there is a clear sense of narrative voice, from whose point of view the story unfolds. As we have seen, *Voices in the Park* experiments with different points of view, and *Captain Abdul's Pirate School* is told through the diary of the fictional Maisy Pickles, whereas Eileen Browne writes *Handa's Surprise* as a first-person narrative using illustration to give us information that is hidden from the main character, Handa. Each of these is a powerful narrative technique with its counterpart in the extended readings of adult fiction.

4. **The use of language.** The language choices, in terms of sentence structure and vocabulary choice, need to be consistent with the narrative elements described above. But they need to combine together to produce readable, interesting and appropriate language. These are difficult ideas to pin down, but at the end of the day our picture books need to read well. One of the best tests for this is to read the book out loud – not the easiest of things for us to do in a crowded bookshop – but the printed text needs to flow, through pattern and repetition, through rhyme or

through a consistent style. The lyrical language of Kit Wright's *Tigerella* is different from the staccato delivery of *Snow White in New York* but both are internally consistent and convey distinct messages that are an integral part of the text as a whole. This holds true for dialogue as well as more sustained prose or rhyme.

5. **The book's values.** All books communicate values and attitudes about the world we inhabit, our society and cultures, whether or not these are directly addressed by the author. There is no such thing as a 'value-free' text. So, in selecting picture books for the classroom we will want to make sure that stories and pictures reflect a range of lifestyles and treat difference and diversity sensitively. It's not simply a matter of avoiding books that contain offensive images or stereotypes (of course this is important) but also one of looking for texts which provide positive images. An increasing number of picture books are now available in dual text format. If you are working in a multilingual school you will probably already be working to include children's home or community languages in the classroom; but children in monolingual contexts can also learn about the languages and scripts used in contemporary Britain, and dual textbooks provide a natural introduction to this sort of learning.

Keeping up to date with picture books

As with any kind of reading, keeping up to date can be a major challenge for us. In our experience, one of the most useful sources is the informal exchange of titles between colleagues and teachers. Keeping in touch with others who are enthusiastic about picture books is highly recommended! 'Have you read . . .' is the stock phrase of any informal reading community. Teachers' Centres, Literacy Centres and Schools Library Services often provide a more structured way of doing this through display, competitions and book lists.

Some teachers are fortunate enough to learn about new books through in-service provision, but many will have to depend on other ways. The magazine *Books for Keeps* is a good source of information, providing useful reviews and other items such as interviews and 'authorgraphs'. *Letterbox Library* is particularly useful for books on equal opportunities issues. Daily newspapers often include features on children's literature and many teachers find *The Guardian* education supplement and *The Times Educational Supplement* useful. It's also worth looking out for the short-lists for book prizes such as the library association's *Kate Greenaway Medal*, the *Carnegie* award and the *Smarties Book Prize*. We provide a list of websites and useful addresses at the end of this book.

Preparing to use picture books

As we saw in Chapter 2, you may have many different reasons for wanting to use a picture book in the classroom. We are keen to stress that there will be occasions on which you will just want to read and enjoy a particular text, and the only real preparation you need for this is your own familiarity with the book you intend to use. If you intend to use a picture book for more formal learning – in the sort of ways we have suggested in the previous chapters – then you will need to be more systematic in your planning.

Given the increased demands on primary teachers and the intense nature of day-to-day classroom life, it is important to be economical in planning and preparing to use picture books. Teachers we have worked with find that making notes on the books and supporting activities is a useful starting point. These notes and ideas can then be kept with copies of the text for future use. The following photocopiable sheet shows our way of looking at what a text has to offer at text, sentence and word levels. This can be used in conjunction with the National Literacy Strategy *Framework for Teaching* (DfE 1998) when selecting the range of texts required for a particular teaching group.

Title

Written and illustrated by

Publisher.   ISBN

Learning opportunities

Range:

Themes:

Terminology:

Outline

Ways of working

Text

Sentence

Word Notes

Extension

Links to Other Texts

Designing activities that encourage a closer reading

Along with the planning sheets, you may want to include examples of activities or games that you have used in conjunction with the text. These may help if you use the same text again or may help colleagues at a later date. In this publication we have restricted our ideas to photocopiable activity sheets. While being aware of the limitations of this sort of activity, it provides a useful vehicle to communicate our approach.

In designing these activities we have had certain principles in mind. These include:

- limiting the activity to a clear learning objective;
- ensuring that the activity involves either thinking about the text or rereading a part or parts of it;
- focussing on both verbal and visual aspects of the texts;
- avoiding the temptation to explore themes that move readers away from the text;
- presenting activities in a variety of different formats which require different kinds of responses;
- designing activities that need as little explanation from the teacher as possible;
- using photocopiables that are reasonably attractive and interesting to look at (without breaching copyright!).

Conclusion

In this chapter we have focussed on the practicalities of developing a classroom approach that raises the profile of good quality picture books. We have looked at ways of critically evaluating texts and have suggested a number of ways in which teachers can keep informed about the availability of new and established texts. The chapter has also provided advice on establishing a collection of book summaries and planning how to use picture books in the Literacy Hour and elsewhere in the school curriculum. We concluded with a look at producing text-related activities, such as the photocopiables included in this book.

List of children's books

Ahlberg, Janet and Allan *It Was a Dark and Stormy Night* Puffin
Ahlberg, Janet and Allan *Peepo!* Puffin
Ahlberg, Janet and Allan *Each Peach Pear Plum* Puffin
Ahlberg, Janet and Allan *The Ha Ha Bonk Book* Puffin
Alborough, Jez *Where's my Teddy?* Walker Books

Bellingham, David *The Book of Mythology* Kingfisher
Bloom, Valerie and Axtell, David *Fruits* Macmillan
Briggs, Raymond *The Snowman*
Browne, Anthony *Zoo* Red Fox
Browne, Anthony *A Walk in the Park* Picture Mac
Browne, Anthony *Changes* Walker Books
Browne, Anthony *Willy the Wimp* Walker Books
Browne, Anthony *Piggybook* Mammoth
Browne, Anthony *Voices in the Park* Doubleday
Browne, Eileen *Handa's Surprise* Walker Books
Burnett, Frances Hodgson *The Secret Garden* Puffin
Burningham, John *The Shopping Basket* Puffin
Burningham, John *Oi! Get off our Train!* Puffin

Cave, Kathryn and Riddell, Chris *Something Else* Puffin
Cole, Babette *Dr Dog* Jonathan Cape
Cole, Babette *Prince Cinders* Collins
Cooper, Helen *Bear under the Stairs* Corgi

Dahl, Roald *Revolting Rhymes* Puffin
Dahl, Roald *Charlie and the Chocolate Factory* Puffin

Filipovic, Zlata *Zlata's Diary* Puffin
Frank, Anne *The Diary of Anne Frank* Puffin
French, Fiona *Snow White in New York* Oxford University Press
French, Fiona *Anancy and Mr Drybone* Frances Lincoln

Garfield, Leon *Shakespeare Stories* Puffin
Green, Roger *The Puffin Classics – Myths and Legends* Penguin

Harrison, Joanna *Dear Bear* Collins
Haswell, Peter *It's Now or Never* Red Fox
Hoffman, Mary *Amazing Grace* Frances Lincoln
Hughes, Shirley *Dogger* Collins

Inkpen, Mick *The Blue Balloon* Andersen Press
Innocenti, Roberto *Rose Blanche* Jonathan Cape

Jaffrey, Madhur *Seasons of Splendour* Pavilion Books
James, Simon *Dear Greenpeace* Walker Books

Kroll, Virginia *Masai and I* Puffin

Linden, Anne Marie and Russell, Lynne *One Smiling Grandma* Mammoth
London, Jonathan *Let the Lynx Come In* Walker Books

Mark, Jan *The Snow Maze* Walker Books
Marshall, Edward and James *Three by the Sea* Bodfey Head
McAffee, Annalena and Browne, Anthony *The Visitors Who Came to Stay* Hamish Hamilton
McBratney, Sam *Celtic Myths* Macdonald
McCaughrean G *Orchard Book of Greek Myths* Orchard
McNaughton, Colin *Captain Abdul's Pirate School* Walker Books
McNaughton, Colin *Boo!* Collins
McNaughton, Colin *Jolly Roger* Walker Books
McNaughton, Colin *Suddenly* Collins
McNaughton, Colin *Have You Seen Who's Just Moved in Next Door to Us?* Walker Books
McNaughton, Colin and Ahlberg, Allan *Help!* Walker Books
Mahy, Margaret *The Great Piratical Rumbustification* Dent
Mahy, Margaret *The Man Whose Mother Was a Pirate* Puffin
Mooney, Bel *The Stove Haunting* Mammoth
Murphy, Jill *Whatever Next* Campbell Books

Noyes, Alfred, and Keeping, Charles *The Highwayman* Oxford University Press

Oberman, Sheldon, and Lewin, Ted *Always Adam* Puffin
Oberman, Sheldon, and Lewin, Ted *The Day of Ahmed's Secret* Gollancz

Pfister, Marcus *The Rainbow Fish* Ragged Bears

Ridley, Philip *Krindlekrax* Red Fox
Rosen, Michael *Little Rabbit Foo Foo* Collins
Rosen, Michael, and Oxenbury, Helen *We're Going on a Bear Hunt* Walker Books

Sendak, Maurice *Where the Wild Things Are* Collins
Scieszka, Jon, and Johnson, Steve *The Frog Prince Continued* Puffin
Scieszka, Jon, and Smith, Lane *The Stinky Cheese Man and Other Fairly Stupid Tales* Puffin

Scieszka, Jon, and Smith, Lane *The True Story of the Three Little Pigs* Puffin
Sheldon, Dyan, and Blythe, Gary *The Whales' Song* Red Fox
Sheldon, Dyan, and Blythe, Gary *The Garden* Red Fox
Steedman, Scott *The Egyptian News* Walker Books

Tomlinson, Jill *The Owl Who Was Afraid of the Dark* Mammoth
Trivizas, Eugene and Oxenbury, Helen *The Three Little Wolves and the Big Bad Pig* Mammoth

Waddell, Martin, and Firth, Barbara *Can't You Sleep, Little Bear?* Puffin
Waddell, Martin *Let's Go Home, Little Bear* Puffin
Waddell, Martin, and Oxenbury, Helen *Farmer Duck* Walker Books
Waddell, Martin, and Benson, Patrick *Owl Babies* Walker Books
Williams, Marcia *Mr William Shakespeare's Plays* Walker Books
Williams, Marcia *Greek Myths for Young Children* Walker Books
Wilson, Raymond *Every Poem Tells a Story* Puffin
Wright, Kit *Tigerella* Hippo
Wright, Kit *Dolphinella* Hippo

Useful addresses

Books for Keeps
6 Brightfield Road
Lee
London SE12 8QF

Centre for English in Education
College House
Collegiate Campus
Sheffield Hallam University
Sheffield S10 2BP

Letterbox Library
2nd Floor
Leroy House
436 Essex Road
London N1 3QP

National Literacy Trust
Swire House
59 Buckingham Gate
London SW1E 6AJ

Reading and Language Information Centre
University of Reading
Bulmershe Court
Earley
Reading RG6 1HY

School Library Association
Liden Library
Barrington Close
Liden
Swindon SN3 6HF

Websites

Carol Hurst's Children's Literature Site
www.carolhurst.com/index

Children's Literature Website
www.acs.ucalgary.ca/~dkbrown/index

Centre for English in Education, Sheffield Hallam University
www.shu.ac.uk/schools/ed/english

National Literacy Trust
www.literacytrust.org.uk

National Year of Reading
www.yearofreading.org.uk

Reading and Language Information Centre
www.reading.ac.uk/AcaDepts/en/ReadLang

References

Chamoiseau, P. (1994) *Strange Words*. London: Granta.

Clay, M. M. (1991) 'Introducing a New Storybook to Young Readers', *The Reading Teacher* **45** (4), 264–73.

Eco, U. (1989) 'Books and literacy: a response to new developments', address to the International Conference, Amsterdam. The Hague: SDU Press.

Ellis, S. and Barrs, M. (eds) (1996) *The Core Book*. London: Centre for Language in Primary Education.

Friedberg, J.B. and Segal, E. (1997) 'Read-aloud clubs: equipping parents to support emergent literacy', *Children's Literature in Education* **28** (3) 127–136.

Graham, J. (1990) *Pictures on the Page*. Sheffield: National Association for the Teaching of English.

Graham, J. (1999) 'The creation of readers, or Mr Magnolia meets the Literacy Hour. Will he survive?', in Goodwin, P. (ed.) *The Literate Classroom*, 65–72. London: David Fulton Publishers.

Graham, J. and Kelly, A. (1997) *Reading under Control*. London: David Fulton Publishers.

Harada, V. (1998) 'Caught between two worlds', *Children's Literature in Education* **29** (1), 19–30.

Holdaway, D. (1979) *The Foundations of Literacy*. Sydney: Ashton Scholastic.

Lambirth, A. (1998) 'Making reading cool', *The Primary English Magazine* **4** (2), 28–9.

Laycock, L. (1999) 'Shared reading and shared writing at Key Stage 1', in Goodwin, P. (ed.) *The Literate Classroom*. London: David Fulton Publishers.

Merchant, G. (1992) 'Supporting readers for whom English is a second language', in Coles, M. and Harrison, C. (eds) *The Reading for Real Handbook*. London: Routledge.

Merchant, G. and Marsh, J. (1998) *Co-ordinating Primary Language and Literacy*. London: Paul Chapman.

Phinn, G. (1992) 'Choosing books for young readers', in Coles, M. and Harrison, C. (eds) *The Reading for Real Handbook*. London: Routledge.

Proust, M. (1994) *On Reading*. London: Penguin Books.

Stones, R. (ed.) (1998) *Children's Books about Bullying*. Reading: Books for Keeps.

Thomas, H. (1998) *Reading and Responding to Fiction*. Leamington Spa: Scholastic.

Wells, G. (1987) *The Meaning Makers*. Portsmouth, N.H.: Heinemann.

Whalley, J. I. and Chester, T. R. (1988) *A History of Children's Book Illustration*. London: John Murray and Victoria and Albert Museum.